FATHERS' RIGHTS

FATHERS' RIGHTS

The Sourcebook for Dealing with the Child Support System

Jon Conine

WALKER AND COMPANY / NEW YORK

First published in the United States of America in 1989
by Walker Publishing Company, Inc.

Published simultaneously in Canada by Thomas Allen & Son
Canada, Limited, Markham, Ontario.

Library of Congress Cataloging-in-Publication Data

Conine, Jon.
Fathers' rights : the sourcebook for dealing
with the child support system / Jon Conine.
p.   cm.
Includes index.
ISBN 0-8027-1074-3
1. Child support—Law and legislation—United States.
2. Desertion and non-support—United States. 3. Child support—
United States. I. Title.
KF549.C66   1989
346.7301'72—dc19
[347.306172]   88-29993

Printed in the United States of America

10 9 8 7 6 5 4 3 2

To my parents, Aubrey and Patricia, for their inspiration and encouragement. To my loving wife, Cynthia, for the twenty-one years she has been at my side. To my children, Kelly and Jon, and my grandson, Jeremy, for just being there.

Contents

———————●———————

Introduction

Fred Johnson was a devoted father and husband. He and Mary
had been married for several years and had two healthy
children to whom they were very close. They both had good
jobs: Fred was an accountant and Mary was a nurse. They had
a brand-new car and lived in a nice house in a middle-class
neighborhood. Everything was going right for the Johnsons.

One day, the Johnsons' world changed. A registered letter
came in the mail. It was from an organization called the child
support enforcement agency. Mary opened the letter and was
stunned. Fred had been named as a defendant in a paternity
action. A woman, Jane Smith, had accused Fred of being one
of the possible fathers of her newborn child.

Fred had never been unfaithful, and told his wife that
this was all a big mistake. Mary was irate and didn't believe a
word of it. She knew that Jane Smith was an attractive young
woman who had worked with Fred. Mary was always a little
jealous of Jane, especially when she accompanied Fred on trips
out of town.

Fred couldn't believe what was happening. Why was Jane
Smith doing this? Why was the state doing this? What right
did the state have to jeopardize his family life for something
that was not even true?

The next few months were humiliating for Fred Johnson.

He was interrogated by the county prosecuting attorney; he was brought before a judge. He was photographed; he was given blood tests. He was treated like a common criminal.

Fred finally won the paternity suit. The blood tests proved that he could not be the father of the child. However, Fred had not gotten off free. The ordeal had deeply affected his family life. He and Mary had been very close over the years. They were not only lovers, they were friends. They shared their deepest feelings with each other. Now they seldom talked. When they did, it usually ended in a fight.

Mary had a problem: The paternity suit had left doubts in her mind about Fred. She couldn't believe that a woman would name a man as the father of her child unless there was some truth to it. She was convinced that Fred had had an affair with Jane.

As the months passed, Fred and Mary grew further and further apart. One night Fred came home from work to find that Mary had taken the children and the new car, and left him. Mary had left a note on the kitchen table, stating that she could no longer stand the emotional stress and wanted a divorce. Fred was devastated and bitter. He was losing his family for something that he did not do.

Fred tried everything that he could think of to find Mary and the children. He frequently called the hospital where Mary worked. He contacted all of Mary's friends and relatives. He advertised in the newspaper. His family was nowhere to be found.

Mary and the children had been gone about three months when Fred received another registered letter from the child support enforcement agency. He looked at the envelope and thought, "What more can they do to me? They can't possibly accuse me of getting anyone else pregnant."

Inside the envelope were several legalistic-looking documents. From what Fred could understand, these documents stated that Mary and the children were receiving public assistance. These documents also mentioned something about him owing $1,500 per month in child support if he didn't take action within a certain period of time.

Fred became very angry and threw the letter away. "Those stupid state employees, they never get anything right. My wife cannot be on welfare; she has a good-paying job. I am not divorced so I don't have to pay any child support. If I had to pay child support, how could they make me pay $1,500 per month? I only take home $1,300 per month. They already took my family from me by accusing me of a crime I didn't commit. I'm not going to make the mistake of getting involved with them again. If Mary and the kids really need money, all they need to do is ask."

The child support enforcement agency never contacted Fred again. One day at work, however, Fred's boss called him into his office. He handed Fred a document. It was a wage garnishment from the child support enforcement agency. It ordered fifty percent of Fred's wages to be withheld for child support due and owed. Fred's boss told him that the company did not tolerate things like this. A garnishment causes a lot of extra work, and hurts the company image. He then handed Fred his paycheck and fired him.

As Fred walked out the door, he glanced at his paycheck. The check was not for half of his wages. It was for half of his wages, minus $400 that the credit union deducted each month to pay for the new car that his wife took. Fred got very angry. "Those stupid people at the support enforcement agency. First, they ruined my marriage. Now, they have taken my wages and managed to get me fired from my job."

On his way home, Fred stopped at the bank to deposit what was left of his paycheck. He stopped at the Employment Security Department to apply for unemployment compensation benefits. He also stopped at the local pub to have a few beers and think the situation over.

Fred decided to call the child support enforcement

agency. It was a waste of time. The support officer not only didn't listen to anything that Fred said; he told him that since he didn't respond to the letter they sent him, he now owed $1,500 a month in child support. Fred admitted that he received some documents in the mail, but he didn't understand them. He also stated that he was afraid to get involved with the agency again. The support officer said that he did not accept excuses. The law was the law.

Fred told the support officer that he didn't care what the law said; it was not fair. He did not leave his wife; she took the kids and left him. He shouldn't have to pay child support because he was not even divorced. Even if he had to pay, he couldn't possibly pay $1,500 per month.

The support officer told Fred that he was wrong on all counts. He informed him that the wage garnishment could be released if he would come into the office to negotiate a repayment agreement. Fred told him to go to hell. There were no longer any wages to garnish. He just lost his job because of the support enforcement agency, and he was going to get a lawyer and sue.

The lawyer was of little help. He explained to Fred that he had done something called "default" according to child support enforcement rules. When Fred did not respond to the letter from the enforcement agency, a default order for child support was automatically established against him. As a result, he owed $1,500 each month in child support, plus $4,500 for the three months that he had been separated from his family. This didn't make a lot of sense to Fred, but he knew that he was in trouble.

The lawyer further explained that he could do nothing about the past—Fred owed the money. He did advise him, however, that it might be possible to go to court and get his future child support payments reduced. Fred asked the lawyer to represent him. The lawyer agreed to handle the case, but required a $500 retainer. Fred was to pay him the next day.

Fred stopped at the bank to withdraw $500 for the attorney. He was informed by the teller that there was no money in his account. The child support enforcement agency had taken every cent. Not only was the money gone, all of the checks that Fred had written bounced. Fred asked what right the bank had to give the child support enforcement agency his money. He was told that it was the law.

Fred did not have the money to cover the bounced checks or to pay the lawyer, so he decided to go to the credit union and get a loan. Fred had learned his lesson, however. He was not going to put this money in the bank.

To Fred's surprise, his loan application was denied. He was told that he had a poor credit rating. His child support obligation had been reported to the credit bureau as a delinquent account. The loan officer indicated that he would be happy to reconsider Fred's loan application if he would settle his debt with the child support enforcement agency. Fred answered, "That was why I needed the money."

The situation was really getting serious. All Fred had left was his weekly unemployment benefits. The amount that he would get wasn't enough to pay his bills, much less get him out of his bind. Besides, the way that things were going, he figured that the child support enforcement agency would find some way to get their hands on that, too.

Fred was exactly right. When he received his first unemployment check, it contained a notice stating that fifty percent of his benefits were being withheld for child support. Instead of $150 per week, his check was for $75. That wasn't even enough to pay the *interest* on his child support debt.

Fred immediately called the child support enforcement agency and explained his problem. He did not have the money to hire a lawyer; he did not even have enough money to live on. The support officer was not sympathetic. He informed Fred that his primary responsibility was to his family, and that he should get a job. Fred stated that he had been fired from his job because of the agency, and that he had no job prospects in the near future. The support officer told Fred that he should have thought about this before he decided not to pay his child support, and ended the conversation.

The only thing left to do was to sell the house and use the equity. Fred did not want to sell the house; he was trying to maintain the family home in hopes that Mary and the children would return to him someday. Now he had no other choice.

Fred listed the house with the real estate agency at a price below market value. Within a very short time, the real estate agency found a buyer. Everything was going smoothly until a title search was conducted on the property. It revealed that there was a child support lien on the house. If Fred sold the house, all of the proceeds had to be applied toward satisfaction of the lien. Fred now had nowhere to turn.

Something such as this could not possibly happen in America, could it? Unfortunately, the answer is yes. Actions, such as these, are taken against fathers many times every day.

During the seventeen years in which I have been in child support enforcement, I have seen fathers by the thousands lose. Some, because they did not want to pay child support. Others, because they did not understand the system. I have seen fathers pay child support faithfully to their former wives every month, and then have to pay a second time to the child support enforcement agency. I have seen men with child support obligations that are larger than their gross income. I have seen men required to pay child support for someone else's children. I have seen men fired from their jobs as a result of child support actions taken. I have seen men forced into bankruptcy. I have seen second families forced into welfare. The list goes on and on.

Child support is a very complex subject, and our nation is building even more complex machines to collect it from fathers. A father must understand the child support enforcement system in order to effectively deal with it. That is what this book is about.

The child support enforcement agency will also be known throughout the book as the agency, the child support agency, and the enforcement agency.

FATHERS' RIGHTS

CHAPTER 1

Child Support: The New Cause

Separation and divorce are hard on every member of the family unit, especially so for the father. This is because our society generally places a distorted value on the role of the father in the parent/child relationship. In many instances, his financial role seems to be his most important commodity.

When divorce occurs, the mother almost always gets custody of the children; it doesn't matter whether or not she is able to support them. When this occurs, the children are legally taken away from the father by court order and given to the mother. In a very real sense, the children are no longer his. After the divorce, the father has little voice in how the children are raised or what happens to them.

Usually, the father's only right is to brief periods of visitation, if it is specified in the divorce decree. Even then, the father really only gets to see his children when the mother allows it. Courts are very reluctant to put a mother in jail to enforce a father's rights to visitation. If he attempts to take the children without the mother's permission, it is a crime called parental kidnapping. The penalty can be jail, and possibly the loss of visitation rights forever.

Even though a father's children are taken away, he is still expected to pay child support. The children, however, are not the ones who directly get the money. Since the mother is the custodian of the children she receives the payments. The mother can spend the money as she chooses. She can spend it on the children, or disburse it in other ways. The father has little control over how the money is spent.

The father is required to pay child support, but there are no requirements that the mother provide for the financial support of the children. Supporting the family is usually considered to be the father's responsibility. The mother's primary responsibility is to care for the children. If the father cannot adequately support the family the government will through welfare.

This is not to say that single mothers do not support their children; many work very hard to do so. Likewise, many fathers who can pay child support don't. The point is that this is the system, and it fails miserably. Society cannot take away a father's rights to his children and expect him to cheerfully pay child support. Society cannot expect a father to make enough money to support two separate households. Society cannot afford to support mothers who choose not to work. Yet, this is what it does.

———————————●———————————

Development of the Child Support Enforcement Program

In decades past, divorce was uncommon. Times have changed. Our society is in an era which has been seen as the breakup of the family unit. The divorce rate is approaching fifty percent. Additionally, almost twenty percent of all children are born out of wedlock. The traditional family unit is being replaced with the single-parent household.

As a result of the change in the makeup of the family unit, domestic-relations issues have become major social problems. The father is not the only one who suffers. Government suffers too. When a mother cannot work, or chooses not to, the government must support her. Child support helps, but it is seldom enough.

The primary welfare program in the United States is called the Aid to Families with Dependent Children (AFDC). This program was developed in the 1930s to provide financial assistance to mothers and children when a father was absent from the home. The original intent of the AFDC program was to assist families when the father died. With the dramatic increase in the number of single-parent families, the AFDC welfare caseload skyrocketed.

This increase placed a tremendous financial strain on government. Something had to be done to help reduce the costs of welfare. That something was the child support enforcement program. The idea behind the program was simple: collect all the unpaid child support on behalf of mothers who are receiving welfare and keep the money.

———————●———————

Child Support:
The Cause

The original intent of the child support enforcement program was strictly financial. It had nothing to do with helping mothers or children, or eliminating poverty; it was merely an effort to help relieve the financial burden on government created by the increasing costs of welfare. Today, that has all changed. Child support enforcement has become a cause. The inadequate payment of child support now is viewed as the major reason for poverty among households headed by single mothers.

This can be explained partially by the very existence of the child support enforcement program. It was one of the few governmental programs that actually made a profit. Therefore, it was easy to justify additional staff and convince legislative bodies to enact harsh laws, to allow the program to collect more from fathers and increase profits.

As the program grew, the dollar amount of child support collections going into the state treasury became significant. It then began to be viewed by politicians as the solution to the problem of poverty among single parent families, rather than just a contributing factor. This line of reasoning was made very clear in 1988 by the federal Department of Health and Human Services in its *Twelfth Annual Report to Congress*, which states, "To a large extent, the problem of welfare in the United States is a problem of the non-support of children by their absent parents."

Women's rights groups also have had a significant impact on the development of the child support enforcement program. Members testified in front of legislative committees and lobbied extensively for tougher laws and higher child support orders. These groups were successful in their efforts, aided by the fact that there were few well-organized fathers' rights groups to tell their side of the story.

Regardless of how it happened, it is now a cause. Nonpayment of child support has become synonymous with poverty in single parent families. In any cause, at least three things tend to occur. First, there is a "good" person and a "bad" person. Second, there is an overreaction on the part of government. Third, there is a tendency to compromise the rights of individuals for the good of the cause.

In this cause, the father is the bad guy. He is the one responsible for the poverty of our nation's youth. He is the reason why the costs of welfare are so high. The solution is to make him pay, the more the better. Because the father is the villain, what his problems are, or what happens to him, is not all that important.

The child support enforcement program has turned into a huge collection machine in support of the cause. Its scope and authority has been greatly expanded. New and more efficient methods have been developed to make more fathers pay, and to make fathers who do pay, pay more. Individual rights have been compromised for the good of the cause.

It is big business, and it is getting bigger all the time. The child support enforcement program has over 29,000 employees nationwide. It has over 10 million cases and collects $4 billion each year. Within the next few years, it can be expected that the child support enforcement program will become involved in all cases of separation and divorce unless the trend is changed. Neither the mother nor the father will have any choice in the matter.

The child support enforcement program has not accomplished its objective; it has not significantly reduced poverty in single-parent households. Less than two percent of the single mothers receiving welfare are removed from the welfare rolls each year because of child support. This is because the nonpayment of child support is not the real cause of poverty in single-parent families. The system is the bad guy. It doesn't work, but the father is being blamed for it.

All fathers have a duty to pay a reasonable amount of child support no matter how badly the system treats them. It is not possible, however, for fathers to ever pay enough to solve the problem of poverty in single-parent households.

This is what the child support enforcement program is attempting to make fathers do, and it is not working.

The real problem is that there is not enough money to go around after separation or divorce. Until the government recognizes this and develops programs to assist mothers in obtaining gainful employment, the problem will never be solved. It is important that mothers who are receiving welfare, and are physically able to work, be required to do so. Equally important, government must create an environment where mothers can work.

This involves the development of training programs to provide the necessary job skills so that mothers can obtain meaningful employment. It also involves the development of affordable day-care programs so that those who do have job skills can work. The lack of affordable quality day-care is a major deterrent to mothers entering the workforce, and is rapidly becoming one of our most significant social problems. Millions of children go without care each day while their parents work.

Some states are attempting to change the system. As an example, Washington State recently enacted a program called the Family Independence Program (FIP) as an alternative to welfare. It does not require mothers to work, but it does emphasize job training and employment, and offers financial incentives for welfare mothers who are willing to go to work. The FIP program also recognizes the necessity of adequate day-care services and pays the cost of day-care to assist mothers in becoming financially independent.

At the federal level, legislation has recently been proposed that, if enacted, would attempt to reform the welfare system on a national level, much like the FIP program in Washington State. It is called the Family Support Act, and does require mothers who are receiving welfare to work under certain circumstances. What the ultimate outcome will be, however, remains to be seen. Many of the provisions of this legislation do not become effective for several years.

Someday welfare reform may become a reality. In the meantime, however, the father is caught in the middle. He must deal with a social environment that takes away his rights to his children and expects him to pay the bill. He must deal with a social environment that is attempting to force him to resolve a problem that he can't possibly solve.

———●———

The Principles Underlying the Cause

Most people do not have a detailed knowledge of the law. People do, however, develop an understanding of their rights and responsibilities in society. They also develop a sense of equity in terms of what can and cannot be done to them. In other words, people develop a concept of fairness. They make decisions based upon what they consider to be fair and right.

In most situations, this learned concept of fairness is an adequate basis upon which to make a decision. Decisions regarding the child support enforcement program, however, cannot be made based upon any concept of fairness. This is one reason why fathers lose. Too often fathers say, "They can't do that to me, it is not right," only to find out too late that they can do it, and did.

There are four principles underlying the child support enforcement program:

1. Primary responsibility
2. Comparative responsibility
3. Burden of proof
4. Default

These principles apply to almost every chapter in this book. The first two principles help explain *why* the child support enforcement program can do what it does. The remaining two principles help explain *how* the child support enforcement program can do what it does.

PRIMARY RESPONSIBILITY

The support of minor dependent children is considered a parent's primary responsibility. Everything else comes second. The financial circumstances of the father are not important. When a child support order is established, the judge does not check the father's credit rating, or outstanding bills, to see what he can afford to pay. When it comes to collecting child support, the child support enforcement program does not take into consideration the father's other financial obligations.

COMPARATIVE RESPONSIBILITY

Either or both of the parents can be made entirely responsible for the support of the children; child support is not a responsibility equally divided between them. This principle makes it possible to shift a disproportionate burden of the cost of supporting the children to either of the parents. If the mother cannot, or chooses not to work, the father may be required to pay the entire bill. Likewise, working mothers must pay the bill if a father does not pay his share of the child support.

BURDEN OF PROOF

In order to collect child support more efficiently, laws have been enacted that shift the burden of proof to the father under certain circumstances. In a sense, this means that the father is guilty unless he proves himself innocent. For example, a father must be able to prove that he made his child support payments or he may have to pay them a second time. The child support enforcement agency does not have to prove that the father didn't make these payments in order to collect.

As will be seen throughout the book, there are several other instances where the burden of proof can be shifted to the father. This principle allows actions to be taken against a father that might not otherwise be taken. It speeds up the process of collecting child support. The child support enforcement agency does not have to know all of the facts of the case before it takes action. The father must provide the facts, or he loses.

DEFAULT

Default is one such case in which the burden is shifted to the father. As will be seen throughout this text, many different types of actions can be taken against a father. In order to take an action, the father must usually be provided with a notice. Once this notice is received, the burden is on the father to respond. If the father does not respond within the time period specified in the notice, he loses by default.

Default is vicious. It is usually the worst thing that can happen to a father. He loses his right to defend himself. And if a father doesn't defend himself, no one else will. (Default will be explained in much more detail in subsequent chapters.)

---●---

Dealing with the System

The social and political environment that fathers are up against is formidable. However, fathers *can* deal with the system and succeed. The key is to understand the system and to actually deal with it. Most fathers lose because they do not understand the system, or they ignore it until it is too late.

In order to succeed, a father must first accept the fact that the child support enforcement program is not fair. It is not there to help him, and there are few protections afforded a father. He must help himself. If a father cannot afford to pay his child support, that is his problem. If a father has problems enforcing his rights to visitation, that is his problem.

A father must also recognize that his problem is with the system, not with his children. The children do not take themselves away from the father, the system does. The children do not take harsh actions against their father, the system does. A father does not succeed by avoiding his responsibility to provide for the financial support of his children. A father succeeds by positioning himself so that he does not lose because of the system.

Likewise, a father is not depriving his children by fighting the system. A father does not penalize his children by obtaining a reduced child support order; he is merely protecting himself. A father can always pay more, but he can't pay less. A father with a $100 child support order can pay $500. A father with a $500 child support order is in big trouble if he cannot afford to make the payments.

Obviously, fathers must understand the rules of the system in order to deal with it effectively. That is what much of this book is about. Understanding the rules, however, is not enough. Fathers must actually play the game. The child support enforcement program is extremely powerful. Its power is matched only by that of the Internal Revenue Service. It cannot be ignored. A father must act, and he must act intelligently.

The game does not begin when a father receives a notice from the child support enforcement agency; it begins the day a father realizes that the marriage is not working. Divorce is one of the most important decisions made in life, and it requires advance planning. Every father of minor children who considers separation or divorce must assume that he will become involved with the child support enforcement agency at some time or other. If a father isn't prepared in advance, he will have much to lose.

CHAPTER 2

———————●———————

The Collection Machine

The child support enforcement program of today is a federal program. It was created in 1975 by the U.S. Congress as an amendment to the Social Security Act. This is the same law that requires individuals to pay into the social security program. It is also the same law under which welfare programs are authorized.

The Social Security Act gives the Department of Health and Human Services responsibility for administering the child support enforcement program, but the states rather than the federal government actually do the work. Every state, however, must strictly conform to the requirements of federal law. This means that all states do much the same thing.

Under federal law, each state is required to establish a single and separate organizational unit responsible for performing the child support enforcement activities uniformly on a statewide basis. This organizational unit is called the state child support enforcement agency. It is the collection machine, and it must perform. If a state does not meet certain performance criteria, the federal government can penalize that state by withholding millions of dollars in welfare funds.

Many of the federal performance criteria that states must meet are procedural. For example, states must attempt to withhold a father's wages in cases where the father is delinquent thirty days or more in his child support obligation. If a state does not do so, it is subject to a penalty. These procedural performance criteria will be explained in detail in subsequent chapters.

Other performance criteria relate to the efficiency in which states collect child support from fathers. For example, states are required to collect a certain percentage of the total child support due each year. They are also required to maintain a certain cost effectiveness ratio, i.e., collect so many dollars in child support for each dollar of administrative expenditure.

In all but five states, this organizational unit is located in the Welfare Department. In Alaska, Massachusetts, and Montana, it is located in the Department of Revenue, and in Hawaii and Texas it is located in the Office of Attorney General. (Appendix A contains a listing of the state child support enforcement agencies.)

The child support enforcement agency does more than just collect child support; it is responsible for ensuring that four primary activities are carried out uniformly on a statewide basis. These activities, which will be discussed in detail in subsequent chapters, are as follows:

1. Locating fathers in child support and parental kidnapping cases
2. Establishing child support obligations
3. Establishing paternity
4. Enforcing child support obligations

The state child support enforcement agency is responsible for the overall operation of the program, but some of the activities may be contracted out to other governmental entities within the state. Most commonly, these activities are contracted out to county prosecuting attorneys. The prosecuting attorney then becomes responsible for establishing and enforcing child support obligations through the judicial court system.

As an alternative, states are beginning to use what is called an administrative process through which to perform child support enforcement activities. Under the administrative process, the child support enforcement agency uses its own staff and hearings examiners, instead of prosecuting attorneys and judges, to establish and enforce child support obligations.

Most fathers pay attention when they receive a notice from a county prosecuting attorney. Everyone knows that prosecuting attorneys are powerful. Fathers, however, often discard a notice from a state employee. This is always a mistake. The administrative process is just as powerful, and often more ruthless, than a judicial process. Remember, the Internal Revenue Service uses an administrative process to collect taxes.

Regardless of whether an administrative or judicial system is used, the activities that must be performed are the same. Also, the processes used to carry out these activities are very similar. From a father's perspective, it amounts to nothing more than who does the work.

Within the child support enforcement agency, there are three programs: the public assistance child support program, the non-assistance child support program, and the foster care recovery program. The four basic activities of the enforcement agency are performed within each of these programs (i.e., locating fathers, establishing child support obligations, etc.). There are some differences in the rules and regulations, but the real difference is where the money goes.

———————●———————

Public Assistance Child Support Program

The purpose of the public assistance child support enforcement program is to reimburse the state for public assistance given to custodial parents and their dependent children. The program makes money for the state by collecting child support and keeping it, and doing it as efficiently as possible.

As a condition of receiving public assistance, the custodial parent, which is almost always the mother, is required to assign all rights to child support to the state. The assignment continues until the mother and children terminate assistance. This means that any monies the father owes, or may owe, for child support now belong to the state. The state then becomes responsible for collecting this child support and keeping a portion of the money as a reimbursement for public assistance paid.

Assume, for example, that a father has a child support order requiring him to pay $300 per month. Assume further that the father owes $3,000 in past-due child support. When the mother and children begin receiving public assistance, the father no longer owes the $3,000 to the mother. He owes the money to the state. In addition, he owes the state the $300 child support payment, each month, until the mother and children terminate public assistance.

There are few defenses against a father's liability to pay for public assistance received by his wife and children. She has the right to say whether or not she wants to receive public assistance. Even if the mother receives public assistance fraudulently, the father still has the responsibility to reimburse the state for the public assistance expended up to the limit of his child support obligation.

This may seem unfair to the father, but it is really not. It is actually a penalty imposed upon the mother for receiving public assistance. As a condition of receiving money from the state, the mother is required to give the state the right to any money owed to her by the father. It does not cost the father any more money, one way or the other. The father is simply paying the state money that otherwise would have gone to the mother. It is the mother who is giving up the money.

THE MOTHER'S RESPONSIBILITY TO COOPERATE

As a condition of receiving public assistance, the mother is also required to cooperate with the child support enforcement agency. Cooperation includes many things, such as testifying at hearings, turning over any child support payments received from the father, etc. For the most part, however, cooperation means providing information about the father. As will be seen in the next chapter, the process of locating the father and his assets begins with the mother. Often, there is little that the agency can do without the mother's cooperation.

If a mother does not cooperate with the agency, her monthly public assistance grant is reduced. Mechanically, her needs are deleted from the grant. A mother and two children would normally receive a public assistance grant for three persons. If the mother fails to cooperate, she would receive a grant for only two persons.

PAYMENT TO THE CHILD SUPPORT AGENCY

Once the mother begins receiving public assistance, the father no longer makes child support payments to the mother; he must make payments to the child support enforcement agency. If a father continues to pay the mother after the agency has notified him that she is receiving public assistance, he may have to pay a second time. Thousands of fathers have learned this lesson the hard way.

A mother may try to deceive the father to get extra money for herself by telling him that she is no longer receiving public assistance, and to make the child support payments directly to her. An unsuspecting father may do so, only to find out later that she lied. He will still be required to make the payment over again to the child support enforcement agency. It may not be the father's fault, but he will get stuck with the bill.

If a father is notified that he is to make child support payments to the child support enforcement agency, he must do so. He must continue to do so until notified otherwise, in writing, by the agency.

WHO GETS THE MONEY

The child support laws were enacted by the same people who make the income tax laws: our members of Congress. As a result, the distribution of child support collected is almost as complex as an income tax return. There are very few people in the child support enforcement agency who will tell a father where his money goes. This is for good reason. There are very few people who actually know where it goes.

Federal law requires that child support payments be divided into two categories. The first is the monthly child support obligation, the amount due each month. This is referred to as current support. If a father has a child support order requiring him to pay $300 each month, the current support is $300. If a father has a child support order requiring him to pay $100 per week, his current support obligation is $100 times 4⅓ weeks in a month; or $433 per month.

The second category is called arrearages. The arrearage is the amount of past-due support. If a father's current support obligation is $300 per month and he is three months behind, his arrearage is $900. Different states use different names to refer to arrearages. Some states call it child support delinquency, others call it past-due child support, or subrogated debt. Regardless, it is the amount that a father is behind in his child support payments.

Any monies collected from the father must first be applied to the current month's child support obligation. Any monies collected in excess of the current month's child support obligation are applied to arrearages. Once this is done, the state must go through a complex distribution process to determine who gets the money.

In order to make the distribution formula as simple as possible, assume that a mother is receiving a welfare grant of $200 per month. Assume further that the father has child support obligation of $300 per month, and that he made a payment of $400 to the child support enforcement agency.

The $400 child support payment made by the father would be divided into current support and arrearages. The father would be given credit for a $300 current monthly child support payment, and a $100 payment on past-due support. The distribution would then be as follows:

1. The first $50 collected each month is paid to the family (the mother and children) without any reduction in their welfare benefits. Based upon the above example, the family would receive $50 from the $300 current child support payment.

2. The current support paid during the month is then compared with the public assistance grant. The state keeps the entire current support payment, except for the first $50, up to the total amount of public assistance paid for that month. If the monthly current support payment is greater than the public assistance grant, the difference is paid to the family.

In the example, the welfare grant was $200. The current child support payment was $300. Because the current monthly child support payment was $100 more than the welfare grant, the family would receive the $100. The family now has $150; $50 from step one, and $100 from this step.

There is $150 left over from the $300 current child support payment. The state gets to keep this $150 as a reimbursement for public assistance.

3. The final step in the distribution process is to compare the arrearage payment with the total amount of public assistance paid since the family has been on welfare. The state keeps all arrearages up to the total amount of unreimbursed public assistance paid. Once all of the public assistance has been reimbursed, any arrearages collected are paid to the family.

In the example, the state would retain the entire $100 arrearage payment if there were $100 or more in unreimbursed public assistance. If there were no unreimbursed public assistance, the entire $100 would be paid to the family.

The distribution process does not stop here. The money that the state keeps is actually divided between the state and the federal government. There is another complex set of rules by which the state does this.

Don't worry if you cannot totally understand the distribution process. It is very complex. The important thing to remember is that the mother assigns all rights to child support to the state when she receives public assistance. From that point on, the state owns any past-due child support owed, plus the current support due each month. When child support is collected it is distributed between the mother and the state based upon federal rules. Neither the mother nor the father have any say in where the money goes.

The formula for distributing child support collections has changed several times over the last few years, and it can be expected to change in the future. In the past, the primary emphasis was to have the state retain as much money as possible. Currently, the trend is to give the mother more of the child support, and for the state to retain less.

PARENTS REUNITING

It is often the case that parents will separate, and the mother and children will go on public assistance. After a period of time, the mother and children terminate from public assistance and reunite with the father. This in no way limits the debt owing to the child support enforcement agency.

Once the parents reunite, the monthly child support obligation stops. Any past-due child support debt, however, continues to exist, and the child support enforcement agency will continue to collect the past-due support up to the total amount of public assistance paid.

———●———

Non-Assistance Child Support Enforcement Program

The child support enforcement agency is required to provide child support collection services to mothers who are not receiving public assistance. This program is called the non-assistance program, or sometimes the non-AFDC program. It was designed as a welfare-prevention program. The idea was to collect child support in non-welfare cases in order to maintain family income at such a level that public assistance expenditures would not be required.

In the past, the primary emphasis was placed on the public assistance child support program. Now that child support has become a cause, much more emphasis is being placed on the non-assistance child support program. The federal government even pays states an incentive payment to collect in these cases. This incentive payment can be as much as ten percent of the amount that is collected by the state. It is not taken from the money collected; that money belongs to the mother. It is given to the state by the federal government.

The non-assistance child support program is not a welfare program. There are no eligibility requirements that must be met, other than the applicant having physical custody of the children. It is open to rich and poor alike. Some states charge the mother a fee for this service and some states charge no fee at all. Some states charge the father the fee. It is entirely possible for the child support enforcement agency to charge the father a fee for taking collection action against him.

WHERE THE MONEY GOES

The activities performed in the non-assistance child support program are the same as those in the public assistance child support program. The difference between the two is where the money goes. In the non-assistance child support program, the money goes directly to the family. The complex distribution rules and regulations do not apply. Basically, the custodian of a minor dependent child need only request such services. The child support enforcement agency will attempt to establish and enforce the child support obligation, and pay the proceeds to the mother.

The process becomes more complicated when the mother is a former public assistance recipient. In these situations, there is often a past-due child support debt owed to the mother and a debt owed to the state. The enforcement agency is required to pay the mother the monthly current support. Any past-due child support collected can either be paid to the mother or kept by the state. It is up to the discretion of the state.

Foster Care Recovery Program

The above programs deal, for the most part, with situations in which the father is absent from the home. The foster care recovery program deals with those situations where the child is absent from the home. Any time a child is away from the home, there is a potential liability on the part of both parents to pay child support.

It is not uncommon for a child to live temporarily with a grandparent or other relative for one reason or another. When a child is absent from the parents, the child becomes eligible for public assistance. It does not require the consent of the parents. The person providing care can receive public assistance on behalf of the child, and the parents then become liable to reimburse the state.

More commonly, a child will be placed in foster care. The purpose of foster care is to help a child overcome a problem, which usually involves a conflict with the parents. In reality, it is another form of public assistance. If a child is placed in foster care, the parents become liable to reimburse the state for the costs incurred, whether the parents voluntarily placed the child in foster care or the placement was ordered by the court.

Once a child is placed into foster care, it becomes the responsibility of the child support enforcement agency to collect from the parents. The primary difference between the foster care recovery program and the other child support programs is that both parents are liable. In a very real sense, both parents are considered "bad guys."

If the parents are married, a child support obligation will be established that both parents are responsible to pay to the state. If the parents are divorced, the father will be required to make his child support payments to the state. Additionally, a child support obligation may be established against the mother. Collection action can then be taken against both parents at the same time.

It is extremely important that parents determine exactly what their financial responsibility is before placing a child in foster care. Foster care can be very expensive. Further, parents are not always told that they will be required to pay at the time their child is placed into foster care. Social workers are often afraid that the parents will not allow the child to be placed in foster care if they know it is going to cost them money. Therefore, since social workers are primarily concerned with the welfare of the child, they may intentionally neglect to tell the parents the costs of placing a child in foster care.

WHERE THE MONEY GOES

In foster care cases, all the money goes to the state. However, the cost of foster care can be less than the amount of the child support obligation. This is especially true when the parents are divorced and both are paying toward the cost of foster care. Some states limit their collection activity to the amount actually expended. In other states, however, the child support enforcement agency can collect more from the parents than the cost of foster care.

If the agency collects more than the actual cost of foster

care, the parents may be reimbursed for the difference on a monthly basis. Alternatively, the extra money can be placed in a trust account for the child. These monies then accumulate until the child is either emancipated or returned to the home. If the child becomes emancipated, the child gets the money. If the child is returned home, the money is refunded to the parents.

CHAPTER 3

———————●———————

Tracking Down Fathers

The primary concern of most fathers is what the child support enforcement agency can do to them. As will be seen, this agency has a great deal of power. It can establish child support obligations; it can put a father in jail; it can take his wages, automobile, boat, stocks and bonds, and even his house. The child support enforcement agency's ability to use this power, however, is dependent upon what it knows about the father.

In order to do anything to a father, the agency must find him. In order to take anything from a father, it must find his assets. The first step in determining what the child support enforcement agency can do, therefore, is to find out what it knows. If a father knows what the agency knows about him, he can determine what type of actions are most likely to be taken against him. A father can then take steps to prevent these actions from occurring, or at least know what to expect.

The process of obtaining information about the father is called *locate*. In the past, most locate activity involved tracking down the father. This is because the threat of jail was the primary mechanism for enforcing child support obligations. In order to put someone in jail, he must first be found.

Today, most child support obligations are enforced by taking the father's assets, most commonly his earnings. Therefore, much of the locate activity now involves searching for assets rather than trying to find the father. Once a child support obligation has been established, assets may be taken even if the father's location is unknown.

Although the child support enforcement agency has extensive resources through which to locate fathers and their assets, the locate activity is still no easy task. It is the most troublesome function that the agency must perform. Attempts are made to locate millions of fathers each year. Often, attempts are made to locate a father several times in a single year.

When the agency is unsuccessful in collecting child support, the reason is usually the inability to locate the father or his assets. The more mobile a father is, the more difficult it is to track him down.

---●---

The Mother

The locate activity begins with the mother. The mother is required to provide the child support enforcement agency with the information that she knows about the father. This information then serves as the basis for beginning the locate activity.

If the mother can identify where the father and his assets are located, verification of the information is all that is required. If the mother knows, or reveals, little about the whereabouts of the father, the search may require extensive tracing that can lead all the way to records of the federal government.

The quality of the information that the mother provides has a great deal to do with the effort that the child support enforcement agency will put into a case. Every child support enforcement agency has many more cases than can possibly be worked. In order to do the most for the greatest number of people, cases are prioritized. Effort is put into those cases with the greatest likelihood of collection. Cases in which the mother does not provide much information about the father usually receive a low priority. If the agency does not have much information to go on, there is little that can be done.

The type of case also has a great deal to do with the quality of the information that the mother provides. In public assistance cases, the quality of information is often poor. This is because most of the money that is collected is kept by the state. There is little incentive for the mother to provide any more information than is necessary to obtain her welfare grant.

In non-assistance cases, the mother gets all the money. Additionally, she is usually out for the father's blood. The mother will provide the child support enforcement agency with all the information she has. If she doesn't know something, she will attempt to find it out.

Because the quality of information provided by the mother is better, the enforcement agency is much more successful in collecting in non-assistance cases. More fathers are located, and collections are made in a greater percentage of cases. There is a much higher probability, therefore, that a father will be located and have child support enforcement action taken against him if his former wife is not on welfare.

———————————●———————————

The State Locate Process

The most critical piece of information needed by the child support enforcement agency is the father's social security number. Without it, locate is extremely difficult. A name does not uniquely identify a person. There are thousands and thousands of individuals named John Smith. In today's society, the social security number is what uniquely identifies one person from another.

A father's social security number gives the child support enforcement agency access to most records, both government and private. Information obtained from government records is usually not as current as information obtained from private sources. Government records are relied on heavily, however, because computer matches can be performed. This greatly reduces the effort required.

Some of the major government locate sources within the state are outlined in the following sections.

EMPLOYMENT SECURITY DEPARTMENT

The employment security department is the primary locate source of every child support enforcement agency. The name may vary from state to state, but it is the department that is responsible for paying unemployment compensation benefits. Businesses must pay this department an unemployment compensation insurance premium for each employee, based upon the employee's earnings. Therefore, records are maintained on where an individual is employed and how much he earns. If an individual is receiving unemployment compensation benefits, records are maintained on the amount he is receiving and his mailing address.

The child support enforcement agency can obtain this information if it has the father's social security number. Many child support enforcement agencies have employment security records on their own computer systems. Obtaining the information is nothing more than typing a name and social security number into a computer terminal.

Information obtained through employment security records is not current. It can be up to six months old. Employers are only required to report this information on a quarterly basis. In addition, employers are given a period of time, usually forty-five days, after the end of a quarter to submit the information. If a father changes jobs frequently, this information is of little value. By the time the child support agency receives the information, the father has moved on to another job.

The employment security department does not maintain records on all individuals who are employed. It only maintains records on individuals who are covered under the government unemployment compensation program. Businesses usually do not pay unemployment insurance premiums for individuals who work under contract. Therefore, records are not maintained on these individuals.

Some of the larger employers self-insure. They assume responsibility for paying unemployment compensation benefits if an employee is fired or laid off. When a business self-insures, the employment security department does not maintain records on the business's employees. Public employees (state and local government employees) are often self-insured. If a father is employed by a self-insured employer, the records of the employment security department will not reveal his employer.

DEPARTMENT OF PUBLIC ASSISTANCE

The child support enforcement agency has access to all public assistance records. These records will provide the current address of anyone who is receiving public assistance benefits, and the last known address of former public assistance recipients. However, this locate source does little more than provide the address of a father. States do not usually take child support collection action against public assistance benefits.

DEPARTMENT OF MOTOR VEHICLES

If the child support enforcement agency has the father's date of birth, it can obtain the home address that is printed on his driver's license. The address is often old, but an old address can lead to a new one.

If the agency can obtain a vehicle's license plate or registration number, it can find the name and address of both the legal owner and the registered owner. Depending upon state licensing laws, this may also include items such as boats and travel trailers, in addition to cars.

Like driver's license information, the information contained on the motor vehicle registration may be old. However, if money is still owed on the vehicle, the legal owner (bank or credit union) will know the current address, because the father is making monthly payments.

DEPARTMENT OF REVENUE

Some states have an income tax and many have a sales tax. In states which have an income tax, employment and residence address information can be obtained from the state income tax return. In those states which have a sales tax, the revenue department can provide the business address of self-employed individuals. Businesses must collect this tax and pay it to the state. The tax department maintains records on each business, and the amount of sales tax that it pays.

PROFESSIONAL LICENSES

Many professions and occupations are licensed or bonded by the state (e.g., doctors, real estate salesmen, beauticians, contractors, etc.). Through the state licensing department, the child support enforcement agency can obtain the current business address of any individual who is licensed by the state. This information is usually current.

U.S. POSTAL SERVICE

The postal service is a federal agency, but it is an often-used locate resource in every state. The postal service is used for three purposes. The first is to verify addresses. If a locate source reveals an address, the postal service can be used to verify it. This saves the child support enforcement agency the time and effort involved in initiating an action when the address is no longer valid.

The second purpose is to find a forwarding address. If the enforcement agency has an old address, it may be able to get the new one through the post office. When individuals move, they often leave a forwarding address so that they can receive their mail, although they are not required to do so.

The third purpose is to find the address behind a post office box. More and more, individuals are using post office boxes to receive mail. In order to obtain a post office box, the postal service requires that the underlying address be provided.

---●---

Private Locate Sources

Private locate sources are usually much more current than government records. However, the child support enforcement agency does not have the same access to private data sources that it does to government records. Most private locate requests must be performed manually rather than through computer matches, and the information is not always given freely. Often, the agency must subpoena private records. Some of the primary private locate sources are outlined in the following sections.

CREDIT BUREAUS AND CREDITORS

While information from most private locate sources must be requested manually, credit bureaus are an exception. Credit bureaus have an extensive national computerized network. Within this network are files that contain the name, last known address, employer, and social security number of almost anyone who has received credit. Additionally, these files contain creditor and credit rating information.

Many child support enforcement agencies have computer terminals in their offices that are linked directly into the credit bureau network. The information is current as of the last time an individual applied for credit.

FRIENDS AND RELATIVES

This can be one of the most productive locate sources. Individuals seldom lose contact with friends and relatives, especially parents. However, since friends and relatives do not willingly provide information to the child support enforcement agency, trickery is often used. A support enforcement officer will call and pretend to be a friend looking for the father, or even an employer with a job offer. The unsuspecting friend will innocently provide the requested information.

UNIONS

If the father is in a trade, hiring is usually done through union halls. If the child support enforcement agency knows a father's occupation and the general area in which he works, it can often trace the employer through the local union. Unions are not always cooperative, however.

FORMER EMPLOYERS

When individuals change jobs, they usually leave the former employer with an address where they can be contacted. At the end of the year, the employer must provide the former employee a W-2 form so that he can prepare his income tax return. The employer cannot do this unless he knows where to contact the worker.

BANK ACCOUNTS

Banks and other financial institutions, such as credit unions, usually have a current address for their account holders. These institutions also hold money in checking and savings accounts that can be taken by the child support enforcement agency.

In order to obtain this information, the child support enforcement agency must first know where a father has his bank account. More than likely, the father already provided this information voluntarily. If a father ever made payment to the child support enforcement agency by personal check, the agency probably already knows where his bank account is and his account number. A personal check contains all the necessary information required to seize a bank account.

UTILITY COMPANIES

Utility companies have very current records on home addresses. In order to provide a service, such as natural gas or electricity, the utility must know where to deliver the service. Some utility companies now allow computer matches with the records of the child support enforcement agency.

Utility companies do not have records on everyone who uses a utility, however. It depends upon who is responsible for the bill. For example, if a father lives in an apartment and the apartment owner pays the utilities, the utility company does not have a record on the father.

———————●———————

Interstate Locate

The locate process becomes much more difficult when a father leaves the state. The child support enforcement agency does not have direct access to government records or private business records in other states. Therefore, it must rely on cooperation from other states, or utilize the Federal Parent Locator Service (FPLS), which will be explained in the next section.

Every state child support enforcement agency is required to have a parent locator service. If one state suspects that a father resides in another state, it will make a request to the other state's parent locator service for assistance. The other state then attempts to locate the father.

Even if a high level of cooperation among states existed—which it doesn't—the interstate locate system would not work well. First, the child support enforcement agency must have an idea into which state the father has moved. Otherwise, requests must be sent to all fifty states. This must be done manually. With over ten million cases nationwide, it is not possible.

Second, a state will only put a minimum of effort into locating a father for another state. Most states will only check records that are computerized. This usually means that the employment security records will be checked. Some states will also check the welfare records. States that have an income tax may check the records of the tax department.

Regardless of the effort that one state will put into helping another state, the data is usually old. It takes time for a state to determine which state the father has likely moved to, and submit a request for locate services. It takes time for the other state to act upon the request and return the information.

Some states are beginning to use interstate computer cross matches. The most common match is with the records of the employment security department. Additionally, the child support enforcement agencies are obtaining computer terminal access to the National Law Enforcement Telecommunications System. This information source provides driver's license, motor vehicle, and criminal information on a nationwide basis.

———————●———————

Federal Parent Locator Service

In 1975, the U.S. Congress passed legislation creating a Federal Parent Locator Service (FPLS) for the purposes of assisting states in establishing and enforcing child support obligations. Later, this service was expanded to include cases of parental kidnapping. States submit over 1.3 million requests to the FPLS each year.

There is a great deal of information available at the federal level on most of the adult population of the United States, and the FPLS has access to most of it. The only information that is not available is that which would contravene the national policy or security interests of the United States, or the confidentiality of census data.

In order to obtain this information, the child support enforcement agency submits a request to the FPLS containing the father's name and social security number. The FPLS then conducts a search of the federal agencies that might have information about the father, and returns the results to the child support enforcement agency.

States can submit cases to the FPLS in instances where the father's social security number is unknown, if at least three of the five following pieces of information are known:

1. The father's date of birth
2. The maiden name of the father's mother
3. The name of the father's father
4. The father's place of birth
5. The social security number of the former wife

The FPLS will then attempt to find a social security number for the father. If successful, a search of federal records will then begin. The success rate in obtaining a valid social security number for the father is, however, very low.

Most frequently, locate information is obtained from the following federal agencies:

INTERNAL REVENUE SERVICE

The Internal Revenue Service (IRS) can provide the child support enforcement agency with any information contained on an individual's income tax return. In addition to the income tax return, the child support enforcement agency has access to the IRS Form 1099 file. This file contains individual asset information. Financial institutions are required to submit a Form 1099 to the IRS each year, stating the amount of interest or dividends paid to individuals. This form also contains the address of the owner of the assets, and the financial institution.

The IRS files contain a wealth of information, but the information is relatively old, since individuals are only required to submit an income tax return once each year.

SOCIAL SECURITY ADMINISTRATION

The Social Security Administration maintains records on how much an individual earns, where he is employed, and how much was paid into the social security trust fund. This information is usually of little value to the child support enforcement agency because it can be eighteen months to two years old.

NATIONAL PERSONNEL RECORDS CENTER

The National Pesonnel Records Center maintains information on all current and retired federal employees. This information is available, and unlike much of the other federal information, it is current.

DEPARTMENT OF DEFENSE

Like the National Records Center, the Department of Defense maintains records on all active-duty servicemen. This information is also current.

VETERANS ADMINISTRATION

If an individual is receiving benefits from the Veterans Administration, this agency can provide the most current address to which these benefits are being sent.

IMMIGRATION AND NATURALIZATION SERVICE

The Immigration and Naturalization Service maintains records on individuals who are legal aliens in the United States. These records contain the home address, employer, and assets of legal aliens.

A Father's Strategy

The child support enforcement agency has access to most information available, both public and private, if it has a father's social security number. It cannot possibly check all of these sources, however. The problem is that a father does not know which of these sources the child support enforcement agency will check and which ones it won't.

Most child support enforcement agencies will check the records of the employment security department, quarterly, in an attempt to find a father's employer. The records of the state Department of Motor Vehicles will be checked if the father's date of birth is available. Additionally, public assistance records will be checked because they are handy. If the child support enforcement agency has an old address, it will attempt to find a new one through the postal service.

This is the extent of the locate activity performed in many cases. Additional locate activity depends upon leads provided by the mother. If she indicates that the father is in the military, then appropriate records may be checked. If she thinks that her husband moved to California, a request will be sent to that state for assistance in locating the father. If all else fails, a request may be sent to the Federal Parent Locator Service.

Because a father does not really know which records will be checked, he must assume that all of these sources will be tapped. A father's strategy then becomes a matter of timing. Most of the information available to the child support enforcement agency is not current. If a father's situation changes more rapidly than the agency receives information, he can assume that nothing will happen. If not, a father knows what to expect.

For example, a father who changes employers every few months can assume that employment security records will not reveal his employer in time for the child support agency to take action. Likewise, a father who frequently moves his money to different financial institutions can assume that federal income tax records will be of little value.

Conversely, a father who is permanently employed must assume that the child support enforcement agency will find that employer sooner or later. A father who has a five year money market certificate in the bank must assume that the IRS records will reveal the certificate.

Subsequent chapters will explain the different types of collection actions that can be taken against fathers. If fathers take the time to compare their circumstances with the locate sources available to the child support enforcement agency, they can determine which types of actions are most likely to be taken against them.

One word of caution: Under no circumstances should a father obtain a new social security number. The loss could be greater than any possible gain. A social security number can be the key to financial security when it is time to retire. Multiple social security numbers can ruin everything.

CHAPTER 4

———————●———————

Temporary Child Support Orders

Once the child support enforcement agency has located the father, it then attempts to take action against him. If the parents are divorced, the agency will attempt to enforce the provisions of the divorce decree. If the parents are not yet divorced, a child support order must first be established.

Parents have a legal obligation to provide for the support of their children. This obligation begins when the children are born, and usually ends when the children reach the age of majority. During marriage, parents satisfy this obligation by providing food, clothing, and shelter for their children.

When a father becomes separated from his family, this obligation continues, regardless of whether or not there is an order requiring him to pay child support. The obligation exists, but it cannot be enforced until an amount is determined. A child support order establishes the amount that the father must pay under the law.

It is important to remember that the obligation to pay child support begins on the day a father becomes separated from his family, not the date in which the child support order is established. Most child support orders, therefore, will require the father to pay child support for a period of time before the child support order was established.

A father can avoid getting stuck with a big bill for past-due child support by paying child support to the mother, even though the amount of his obligation has not yet been established. However, if too much is paid, the excess amount will not be returned. Therefore, it is often better to pay a small amount and put the remaining money in the bank until the amount of the obligation is established.

———————●———————

Establishing Temporary Orders

Parents do not usually get divorced immediately. It may be years from the time of separation until the divorce becomes final. During this interim period, some sort of an order for child support must be established. These interim orders are called *temporary orders*. A divorce decree deals with many issues other than child support, such as visitation and property settlements, and possibly alimony or spousal maintenance. A temporary order, however, usually only deals with child support–related issues.

The child support orders that the enforcement agency establishes are temporary orders. These orders only remain in effect until a divorce decree is entered, which then replaces the temporary order. From that point on, the child support enforcement agency will enforce the divorce decree.

A divorce decree replaces a temporary order in terms of the monthly child support obligation. However, it does not necessarily forgive the father from the responsibility to pay any amount still owing under the temporary order. If the father has not paid the entire amount of the temporary order, the child support enforcement agency can probably collect it.

Temporary orders can be established through the court system or through an administrative system. The process is much the same. The difference is that the court system involves a judge, and the administrative system involves administrative hearing officers.

The process of establising a temporary order begins with a notice to the father. The concept of the notice is extremely important. In order to establish a child support obligation, the father must usually be given notice, which is usually provided by personal service or by certified mail. Personal service means that someone actually hands the father the notice. Certified mail is a special type of mail in which the father, or household member, has to sign a receipt. In either case, the agency has a record that the father received the notice.

There are four important parts to this notice, as follows:

1. It notifies the father that the child support enforcement agency is involved in his case.

2. It notifies the father that he has an obligation to support his children, and contains an amount proposed as the monthly child support obligation. The notice may also contain an amount proposed as past-due support.

3. It contains information regarding the father's rights in the process of establishing the child support obligation.

4. It specifies a certain number of days in which the father has to respond to the notice, or a child support order will be established against him by default.

In some cases, the notice will contain a statement that all child support must be paid directly to the enforcement agency. A father may not get credit for any payments made directly to the family after receipt of the notice; however, he is entitled to credit for all payments made prior to receipt of the notice. If he pays any money to the family after receipt of the notice, he may have to pay the child support enforcement agency a second time.

Once the father has received the notice, the burden of proof is shifted to him. It is up to the father to respond and prove why the amount of child support stated in the notice should not be ordered. As explained in chapter one, shifting the burden of proof is a very powerful tool. One of the most common mistakes that fathers make is not responding to the notice, which affords the father his rights to due process under the law. If he does not respond to the notice he is giving up his rights.

After the father has been given proper notice, action is then taken to establish the temporary order. There are three ways in which an order can be established: default, consent, and hearing. Because the notice shifts the burden to the father, his actions determine which type of order will be established.

DEFAULT ORDER

Mr. Jones was a construction worker, and he had made big money over the last several years. New construction activity had begun to slow down, however, and Mr. Jones suddenly found himself unemployed. This not only placed a financial burden on the family, it put a severe strain on the marriage. The strain became so great that he and his wife finally separated.

Mrs. Jones and the children had no choice but to apply for welfare. She did not have a job, and Mr. Jones had no money to give her. He could hardly support himself, as his only source of income was an occasional odd job.

About a month after they separated, Mr. Jones received a notice in the mail from the child support enforcement agency. It stated that his wife and two children were receiving public assistance and that he was financially responsible for their support. Based upon his prior earnings record, the agency had determined his obligation to be $800 per month. The notice also stated that he had twenty days to object, and if he did not do so, he would owe the money.

Mr. Jones did not pay much attention to the notice, and he did not bother to mail in the objection. He had received many bills in the last few weeks, none of which he could afford to pay. It didn't seem to matter, however, because he heard nothing more from the child support enforcement agency.

About a year later, activity in the construction industry began to increase and Mr. Jones finally went back to work. Then it happened. When he received his first paycheck, he found that the child support enforcement agency had taken half of it. And he owed $9,600 in child support for the previous year.

Mr. Jones's case is one in which a default order for child support was entered against him. It is usually the worst type of order. It is also the easiest for a father to get. If he does not respond to the notice within the required time period, a default order is automatically entered against him. The amount stated in the notice then becomes the amount of the child support order.

This is what happened to Mr. Jones, and it cost him dearly. If he had responded to the notice, his child support obligation would not have been $800 per month. The fact that he was unemployed would have been taken into consideration and his obligation adjusted accordingly.

It is very common for fathers to fail to respond to the notice. In many instances, it is because they do not understand its importance, or what will happen to them. In other instances, however, fathers think that the amount stated is what they will be required to pay and that therefore, there is no point in objecting. This is not necessarily the case. The amount stated in the notice may be nothing more than a number that someone pulled out of the air; the child support enforcement agency can put whatever amount it wants in the notice. Since the burden is on the father to show that he should pay less than asked for, little effort is expended into researching a father's financial circumstances.

If the mother is receiving welfare, the notice is often for the amount of the monthly welfare payment. If she is not receiving welfare, it may be for whatever the mother would like to have. Both of these are usually more than the average father should have to pay. There have been cases where default orders have been established that require the father to pay more than he earns.

A default order can be modified downward to reduce the child support obligation, but it may be only prospectively; i.e., the child support order can be modified only with respect to future child support payments. The father is generally liable for the past-due child support that has accrued prior to the modification.

For example, assume a default order was entered against a father for $800 per month in child support. Assume further that the order was modified prospectively five months later to reduce the child support to $300 per month. After the order is modified, the father's monthly child support obligation would only be $300 per month. However, he would still owe the $800 per month for the five months in which the original order was in effect.

A default order can be beneficial if the child support enforcement agency grossly underestimates the father's income, which would result in a reduced child support obligation. However, it is uncommon. The practice is to put an amount in the notice that is much more than the average father would be ordered to pay.

Some states have laws that allow a father who does default a right to a late hearing under very limited circumstances. If a father qualifies, he may be able to get his child support obligation reduced retroactively. *But fathers should never count on this.* Chances are they will not win. The best strategy is not to default in the first place. However, if a father has already defaulted, he should contact the child support enforcement agency, and, if he feels he needs one, an attorney, to find out what his rights are.

CONSENT OR AGREED ORDER

While order by default is usually the worst of all orders, an order by consent can be the best. This is a situation where the father responds to the notice and comes to agreement with the child support enforcement agency on all terms. An order is drawn up and signed by the judge, or administrative hearings officer, without a formal hearing.

It is during the process of developing an order by consent that the father has the greatest flexibility in terms of negotiation. A hearing is expensive for the agency, and the staff may be willing to negotiate a deal and avoid the expense. A hearing can also be costly for the father, especially if he must hire an attorney to represent him.

HEARING ORDER

If the father responds to the notice within the required time period, and cannot work out an agreement, he has the right to a hearing. The judge, or hearings officer, will listen to the facts of the case and determine the father's child support obligation.

A father loses much of his ability to negotiate when an order is established through the hearings process. The hearings officer makes the decision. Officers have considerable discretion in what they can order, and often deviate from established child support schedules. This may work in the father's favor, but it may also work against him. At any rate, there is an element of the unknown.

A father has a right to appeal the decision if he is not satisfied. An appeal is nothing more than a request that a higher authority review the decision. The appeal procedures, however, vary from state to state. Instructions on the appeal process should be provided to the father with the initial decision. It is important to remember that the father must begin the appeal process within the time period specified, which is typically twenty to thirty days. If a father is not given the necessary information, he can obtain it from the child support enforcement agency.

Amount of the Temporary Order

Child support orders establish the minimum amount that fathers must pay under the law. Fathers can always pay more, but they can't pay less. There are certain circumstances in a divorce action where it is beneficial to have a high child support order. This will be explained in the next chapter. In temporary orders, however, the father wants to get the lowest total child support obligation possible.

A father is not cheating his children by obtaining the lowest possible temporary order: He can pay as much as he wants for the support of his children. The order merely states a minimum amount that the father must pay before the child support enforcement agency comes after him. The lower the minimum, the fewer problems a father will have.

Generally speaking, there are four parts to a temporary order: the monthly child support obligation, the past-due child support, the payment on the past-due support, and medical insurance. These determine the total amount of the obligation, and the manner in which a father must pay it.

THE CURRENT SUPPORT OBLIGATION

The current support obligation is the amount of child support that the father will be required to pay each month. Every child support enforcement agency is required to have a schedule upon which the current obligation is established. Usually, schedules are based upon the income of the father, or the combined income of the parents.

Child support schedules serve as a starting point in determining the amount that a father must pay. Special circumstances of the father and the children must also be taken into consideration. As an example, a financial hardship on a father, due to large medical bills incurred by the family, would probably be a reason for reducing the obligation. Likewise, a severe illness of a child could be reason to order a father to pay more than the amount required under the schedule.

A father's ability to negotiate a monthly child support obligation that is less than the scale requires a showing of circumstances that cause a financial hardship. One of the best ways to show financial hardship is to itemize monthly income and expenses.

THE AMOUNT OF PAST-DUE SUPPORT

Most temporary orders will contain an amount for past-due child support that the father must pay. As stated previously, a father's child support obligation begins on the date he separates from his family. The child support order, however, is not established until some time later. The past-due child support represents the amount that should have been paid during this interim period.

While a father is responsible for paying child support from the date he leaves his family, a different date may be used to begin the child support obligation. In welfare cases, the date that the mother began receiving welfare is often used. In non-welfare cases, it may be the date that the mother applied for support enforcement services. This works to the father's benefit. Both of these dates occur after the separation. Therefore, the child support debt is smaller.

The amount of past-due support stated in the notice is usually detemined by multiplying the monthly child support obligation by the number of months in which the father did not pay, but the figure may not be accurate. For instance, the father's income may have been lower in prior months, and this should be taken into consideration. A father must raise the issue, and provide proof of earnings, as the enforcement agency is not going to do it.

A father is entitled also to credit for any money that he has provided to his family. Additionally, he may be due credit for such things as making the house payment or providing clothes for the children. Each state varies in what will be accepted as credit against the child support obligation. Again, the father must raise the issue and provide proof. Remember, however, that credit may not be given for payments made directly to the family after receipt of the notice from the child support enforcement agency.

There is much more of an opportunity for a father to negotiate on the past-due amount than on the monthly child support obligation. The primary concern of every child support agency is the establishment and collection of the monthly support obligation. Any monies collected on past-due support are an added bonus. Since much of the past-due support is never collected, the child support enforcement agency may be willing to forego a portion of past-due support in order to avoid the expense of a hearing.

Also, it is not uncommon for the enforcement agency to reduce the amount of past-due child support debt in return for a higher monthly obligation. If the divorce will not be final for a long period of time, this is a bad arrangement. If the divorce will be final in the very near future, however, it may work in the father's favor.

For example, assume that a father agreed to a monthly child support obligation of $100 per month more than he would normally be required to pay in return for a $1,000 reduction in the amount of past-due support. Assume further that the divorce will be final in two months. In the divorce decree, the monthly child support obligation may be reduced to what it should have been. The father saved the $1,000 in past-due support by agreeing to pay $100 extra in current support for two months. The net savings is $800.

PAYMENT ON THE CHILD SUPPORT DEBT

Once the amount of the child support debt is established, there is considerable flexibility on how it is to be paid. Federal law requires that the father pay the entire amount of the current monthly obligation. Payment on the past-due support, however, is up for negotiation. The manner in which the father is required to pay is as important as the amount.

If the debt is substantial, the temporary order will provide for some sort of payment plan. The amount of the monthly payment is negotiable. It is usually based upon the father's ability to pay and the statute of limitations, which involves a period of time past which the father is forgiven for the child support debt. The child support enforcement agency will not want to extend the repayment plan beyond that time period, or it will lose the money. The statute of limitations is explained in chapter eight (see page 129).

All states have the authority to charge interest on child support debts. Some states routinely charge interest while others do not. If a state does not do this, a repayment plan can be a good deal since it is basically an interest-free loan. If interest is charged, the repayment plan may not be such a good arrangement, depending upon the interest rate that is being charged. The higher the interest rate, the more consideration the father should give to borrowing the money and paying off the debt.

If a father is going to make monthly payments on the child support debt, it is important to know exactly what will happen if a payment is missed. There are two possibilities. Either the father becomes delinquent by the amount of the payment missed or the entire debt becomes due immediately.

The child support enforcement agency would much prefer that the father pay his child support debt as a lump sum. Maintaining accounts and processing payments is expensive. Furthermore, child support debts are not usually collected in full. Many states, therefore, will accept a smaller lump sum as payment for the entire debt. It is not uncommon for the enforcement agency to accept a lump sum payment of only fifty to seventy-five percent of the amount owed. This can be a big savings for the father, even if he has to borrow the money to pay the debt.

MEDICAL INSURANCE

The federal government now requires that all orders for child support contain a provision that the father provide medical insurance for his children, if it can be obtained at a reasonable cost. For the most part, this means that a father must provide medical insurance if it is available through his employer.

At the time of writing this book, no state has done much to implement this new federal law. Most new child support orders do contain the statement that the father must provide medical insurance, if it doesn't cost too much. While it is not presently enforced, someday it will be. A father must always assume that every provision in a child support order will be enforced when negotiating terms and conditions. Federal law also states that a father's child support obligation cannot be reduced because of the requirement that he provide medical insurance. In practice however, if medical insurance is paid for by the father, it should be possible to have the monthly child support obligation reduced.

---●---

Stepparent Liability

Ed was on the rebound from a divorce when he met Sharon, a divorcee with four children. He had been lonely for some time and needed a companion, and she seemed to fulfill that need. Likewise, Sharon needed someone to help her with the children, and Ed was good to them; it was very difficult, both financially and emotionally, for her to raise four children alone. Because of their common needs, it was not long before Ed and Sharon were married.

It became apparent in a very short period of time that they had acted too hastily. The marriage was a mistake, and neither Ed nor Sharon was happy. One day, Ed came home from work to find that Sharon and the children had gone. She left a note saying that she was running away with another man. Ed's ego was a little bruised, but he was not all that sorry. Something had to happen sooner or later.

However, Sharon had not told Ed the whole story. She did run away with another man, but she also placed her four children in foster care before she did so. Ed found this out the hard way; he received a notice from the child support enforcement agency a few months after the separation, which stated that the children had been placed in foster care and that he was liable for their support. In the end, Ed was forced to pay for the cost of foster care for his wife's children while she was off having an affair with another man.

What happened to Ed may not seem fair, but some states have enacted laws that make custodial stepparents legally responsible for the support of their stepchildren. When a man marries a woman who has custody of her children, he becomes a custodial stepparent. This does not just apply to men. A woman who marries a man who has custody of his children is also a custodial stepparent, and may be required to pay child support if she separates from the father.

The process of establishing a child support obligation against a custodial stepparent is the same as that of a natural parent. The difference is that the stepparent only has to pay until the divorce is final. He, or she, is then relieved of the obligation. Anyone considering becoming a stepparent should first find out about the laws regarding stepparent liability in his or her state. If the marriage fails, he must file for divorce immediately and have the divorce finalized as soon as possible.

ADOPTIVE PARENT'S LIABILITY

Unlike a stepparent's obligation which ends when the divorce is final, the case is not the same with an adoptive parent.

When a father adopts, the child becomes his under the law, and the obligation to provide for the support of an adopted child continues after the divorce.

Many men adopt their stepchildren without considering the possible consequences. A lifetime commitment is being established. Before adopting, a father must be fully aware of the implications. Almost fifty percent of all marriages end in divorce. This means that there is a fifty-fifty chance that a man who adopts his wife's children will be paying her child support at some time in the future.

CHAPTER 5

———————●———————

The Divorce Decree

A divorce decree is different from a temporary order in two respects. First, it deals with many issues other than child support. A divorce decree dissolves the marriage, establishes custody and visitation rights, and distributes the assets of the marriage between the couple.

Second, a divorce decree is of much longer duration than a temporary order. The terms of the decree must be written so that they continue to apply over a period of years, and the wording must clearly reflect the intent of the parties so that disputes will not arise. A temporary order may only be in effect a few months. Terms of a divorce decree, however, may be in effect for eighteen years, until the children reach the age of majority.

Put simply, a divorce is the dissolution of a business partnership. The terms of the divorce decree specify who gets what, and who has to pay which bills. The children represent some of the assets of the business, and child support is one of the bills.

A divorce is one of the most stressful and emotional times in life. There is a tendency for the individuals involved to be controlled by their emotions rather than logic. Often a father will say, "She can have everything, I just want out." She gets everything, and he lives to regret it. A father must be able to look at the situation rationally and determine what is best for him and his children. If at all possible, it is best to postpone the divorce until both the husband and wife have had a period of time to "cool off."

The divorce decree is much like a contract. It is a document that puts in writing the terms and conditions under which the business of marriage will be dissolved. Planning is the key to a successful divorce. If a father obtains a divorce decree he can live with he may never have any problems. If not, he will have major problems.

The methods for establishing a divorce decree are much the same as that for temporary child support orders. A father can default and all of the issues relating to child support, visitation, and the property settlement will be decided without him. The husband and wife can fight it out in court, in which case the judge makes all the decisions. Or it can be a negotiated agreement, subject to the judge's approval. A negotiated agreement is usually better for all parties concerned.

The mechanical process of obtaining a divorce is best left to attorneys. They understand the court system and know how to complete all of the necessary forms. Too often, however, fathers leave everything to their attorneys. This is a mistake. Attorneys can assist fathers in obtaining divorces, but they are not in the business of planning for their clients' future. Fathers must do that for themselves. The terms and conditions of a divorce decree are a father's future, and those relating to child support are among the most important.

The child support obligation is not just a number that an attorney puts in the appropriate box in his preprinted divorce decree forms. It is a long-term financial commitment, and must be treated as such. It is the obligation that fathers have the most problems meeting. This is why the child support enforcement program exists.

The issue of child support is particularly complex because it relates to every other term and condition contained in the divorce decree. Too often, however, child support is treated as a separate issue. When this happens, the entire family loses.

●————

Divorce Decrees and the Child Support Enforcement Agency

The child support enforcement agency does not become directly involved in divorce actions unless the mother and children have received welfare. Even then, its involvement is usually limited to the child support obligation. Most of the other terms of the divorce decree are left to the parents, or the parents' attorneys, and the judge.

If the mother and children are receiving welfare at the time of divorce, the child support enforcement agency will want the obligation established in the divorce decree to be as high as possible. The money belongs to the state as long as the mother continues to receive welfare.

If there is any past-due child support debt owing at the time of the divorce, the agency will also want to ensure that the debt is not lost when the divorce decree is established. In some states, the agency must become a party to the divorce action in order to preserve the debt. In other states, the debt is automatically preserved under the law. The result is the same: the father continues to owe the debt.

In one sense, the child support enforcement agency should not become involved in any divorce actions. It is an infringement upon the basic rights of both parents. In another sense, the state must protect its rights because some people do cheat the system.

One of the most common examples of cheating the system is divorcing to obtain a second income. The parents will pretend to separate. The mother and children will go on welfare and receive $400 per month plus medical and dental coverage and food stamps. The parents will then divorce and try to obtain a child support order of $50 per month. If the parents are successful, the family has a second income. The father pays $50 per month, and the family receives $400 per month plus all the other benefits.

---•---

Wording the Divorce Decree

The terms and conditions of the divorce decree are extremely important. However, the wording of the divorce decree can be even more important. If the wording does not specifically state what was intended, the result may not be what either party wants. Poor wording is the most common mistake made in divorce decrees today.

The parents may be in complete agreement as to the meaning of each term and condition contained in the decree at the time of divorce. Over a period of time, however, two things tend to happen. First, the parents forget what was intended. Second, circumstances change, and the parents will want to interpret the terms of the divorce decree to best fit their new circumstances.

In either case, there is a dispute, which is handled just like a disagreement over the terms of any other contract. A judge will make a decision based upon the wording of the divorce decree, and not upon intent. There are two parties standing in front of him with two different stories. The wording of the divorce decree is all the judge has upon which to make a decision.

The wording mistakes that cause the most problems are those relating to child support and visitation. These are the terms of the divorce decree that are in effect for the longest period of time. Therefore, they are the most likely to be disputed as the years pass.

As an example, many fathers have lost because the divorce decree does not specify child support on a "per child" basis. Instead, a father is ordered to pay a certain amount "for the support of the children." What happens when one of the children reaches the age of majority? What happens if one of the children decides to live with the father? If the divorce decree is not specific, the father would probably have to continue to pay the entire amount of child support stated in the divorce decree despite the changes in the circumstances.

A correctly worded divorce decree will specify child support on a "per child" basis. Then, there is no question. If one child reaches the age of majority, or comes to live with the father, the child support obligation is reduced by the amount the father was required to pay for that child.

Improperly worded terms regarding visitation can have equally bad results. Many divorce decrees state that the father is entitled to "reasonable rights of visitation." This is also meaningless. At the time of divorce, both parents may be in complete agreement regarding visitation. A few years later, the mother may remarry and not want to have the children see the father. She may decide that reasonable visitation means one day a year. All the father can do is go back to court and have the judge determine what "reasonable" means. This problem can usually be avoided by clearly specifying the visitation times in the divorce decree.

Child support and visitation are the most often disputed terms of a divorce decree. Care must be taken to ensure that all of the terms in the divorce decree state exactly what was intended. Don't count on a lawyer to take care of the wording by himself. The fact of the matter is that most divorce decrees are written by lawyers, and many of them are worded poorly.

One way to help ensure that a divorce decree is worded properly is to go through a "what if" exercise for each term and condition. Try to imagine all of the situations that could possibly occur, and ask, "What if this happened?" If a situation is not specifically addressed, rewording or additional language is necessary. Do not overlook *any* possibilities; a divorce decree is in effect for a long period of time.

---●---

Child Support Schedules

The first step in determining the amount of the child support obligation is to obtain a copy of the schedule currently being used used by the court. The schedule and instructions for its use can be obtained from the court clerk. It will provide a "ballpark" estimate of what a judge would order for child support in that particular county.

No one really knows how much a father should pay in child support. There are literally hundreds of child support schedules in the United States, and every county in a state may use a different schedule. In addition, the one that the enforcement agency uses in setting temporary orders may be different than all the other county schedules.

Most child support schedules are based upon the father's income, possibly the mother's income, and the number of children. Some schedules use gross income; others use net income. Gross income is the total amount of earnings before any deductions. If a father is earning $2,000 per month before deductions, his gross income is $2,000 per month. If he is paid by the week, his monthly gross income is 4⅓ times the weekly gross income.

Net income is not necessarily the amount a father takes home in his paycheck. It is most often defined as gross income, less mandatory deductions. Mandatory deductions are those that are required to be deducted by law. Examples of these deductions are state and federal income tax, social security payments, and mandatory retirement programs. Other deductions, such as credit union payments and life insurance, are not taken into consideration.

It doesn't really matter whether the child support schedule is based on gross or net income. A scale based on gross income does not necessarily require a father to pay more than one based on net income. It is the proportion of income required by the schedule that determines the amount of the child support obligation. The larger the percentage, the higher the child support order.

A simple child support schedule might require a father to pay twenty percent of net income for one child, twenty-five percent for two children, and thirty percent for three children. In this example, a father with two children and a net income of $1,000 per month would owe $250 per month in child support; a father with three children would owe $300 per month.

———————————●———————————

Determining the Child Support Obligation

The amount of child support determined by using the schedule is only a starting point. There are many other issues that must be addressed in a divorce decree, and child support is related to each of them. The amount of the support obligation determined according to the schedule should be adjusted upward or downward based upon the decisions made regarding the other terms and conditions.

More and more, states are attempting to separate the issue of child support from the other terms of a divorce decree. This may help government, but is an infringement upon the rights of the parents. The best arrangement, for all parties, can only be made by examining all of the assets and liabilities of the marriage and working out an agreement that best fits the circumstances of all concerned.

PROPERTY SETTLEMENT

If the parents have been married for a period of years, there may be a substantial amount of property involved. This includes things such as the family home, cars, boats, investments, and so on. At the time of divorce, these assets must be divided between the couple.

Each state has different laws regarding the division of property between the parents. Some states have an equal distribution, an exact fifty-fifty split. Some have an equitable distribution, which is almost a fifty-fifty split. The list goes on. Regardless, the actual distribution of property in an agreed divorce settlement is subject to negotiation between the parents.

It is often better for the father to agree to a higher monthly child support obligation in return for a greater percentage of the property. This is because child support orders are subject to modification. At any time, it is possible for the child support obligation to be increased. The higher the initial child support obligation, the less the likelihood that it will be increased.

For example, assume that the child support schedule indicates that a father should pay $300 per month in child support. Assume further that the division of property was equal. Under these circumstances, the father would normally be ordered to pay $300 per month in child support, and would receive one-half of the property. If the father later received a substantial pay raise, the mother could have the child support obligation modified upward.

Alternatively, it may be possible to work out an agreement to pay $500 a month in child support in return for seventy-five percent of the property. The additional property that is acquired may more than offset the increased child support payments. More importantly, the father does not have to worry about having his payments increased every time he receives a pay raise. He is already paying much more than the schedule requires.

Such a situation may also be better for the mother. She will have a regular monthly income much higher than would have otherwise been possible. She doesn't have to gamble upon future uncertainties that may occur. She may only be giving up assets that she didn't want, or couldn't afford to keep. The forced sale of assets in a divorce situation is frequently a losing situation for both parents.

Alternately, the mother may want to keep a greater percentage of the property for a reduced child support obligation. Most often this happens when she wants to keep the family home. This can signal a potential drain for the father, who in essence is asking to have his child support obligation modified upward at a later date.

A much better solution is to require the mother to make payments to the father for the property, or for the father to hold an interest-bearing note payable in a certain number of years. The net effect is the same as reducing the child support obligation. The father, however, does not have to worry about having his child support order increased.

IRS DEDUCTIONS

One or the other of the parents will probably be awarded federal income tax deductions for the children. This deduction is almost $2,000 per child. Depending upon the income tax bracket of the father, it may be worth paying a little more child support in return for the deduction. Alternatively, it may be more beneficial for the mother to accept a little less in child support in return for the IRS deduction if she is in a high income tax bracket. Again, both parents can reach an equitable solution by taking the time to plan.

VISITATION

The interrelationship between visitation and child support is commonly overlooked when a divorce decree is being drafted. Fathers are actually providing for the financial needs of their children during periods of visitation. Very seldom, however, do divorce decrees contain a provision for reducing fathers' child support obligations while the children are in their care.

If a father has his children once a month, or every other weekend, it probably shouldn't affect the amount of the child support obligation. However, what if the divorce decree specifies that the father has the children for three months in the summer? What if the mother gets sick and the father must take the children for a period of months? A father should be entitled to credit against his child support obligation under these circumstances. It must be specified in the divorce decree or the father may not get credit.

There can also be significant travel expenses related to visitation. The mother may take the children and move across the United States. Visitation then requires someone to pay several hundred dollars for airline tickets. Who picks up the expense? Probably the father does, if he wants to see his children, unless it is specified otherwise in the divorce decree.

Situations such as these reinforce the importance of performing "what if" exercises on the proposed wording of a divorce decree. The divorce decree must be written so that it remains applicable when changes occur.

MEDICAL INSURANCE

Federal law requires that all divorce decrees contain a provision for medical insurance, if the father can obtain such coverage for the children at a reasonable cost. This is the same requirement that was discussed in chapter four for temporary orders. However, because a divorce decree is in effect for a much longer period of time than a temporary order, more attention must be given to the medical insurance provisions.

A father may have an employer who will provide medical insurance for the children at no cost; everyone would agree that "free" is a reasonable cost. Over a period of time, the father may find a new job that does not provide medical insurance. Purchasing a medical insurance policy can cost $150 per month, or more. This may seem like a reasonable cost to the mother, but it certainly won't to the father.

The divorce decree should never contain a term such as "reasonable cost" without defining it. The maximum that the father can be required to pay for medical insurance must also be stated.

If the mother is working, and has medical insurance of her own, there is little necessity for the father to provide additional insurance. If the mother is not working, medical insurance becomes much more important, as all children deserve adequate medical attention.

A father is at a real disadvantage, however, when it comes to negotiating medical insurance requirements because states have not yet developed programs to implement the federal law. Divorce decrees are now requiring fathers to provide medical insurance, but no one really knows what this means. With a temporary order fathers may never have to pay. A divorce decree is in effect for such a long period of time that fathers are forced to deal with the issue.

Because of the uncertainty involved, it is probably best to attempt to minimize the liability for medical insurance in the divorce decree. Should it become necessary, a father can always provide additional medical insurance coverage for his children.

DAY-CARE EXPENSES

If the mother works and the children are small, there will be day-care expenses. It is becoming increasingly common for divorce decrees to require the father to participate in the cost of day-care and a father must be very careful to limit his liability.

To a large extent the costs of day-care are under the control of the mother. She can obtain the most inexpensive day-care possible, or place her children in a very expensive specialized day-care center. She may even work out a "special arrangement" to pay a relative $2,000 per month to watch the children. If the divorce decree does not specify a maximum that a father must pay, he may get stuck with a large bill.

The divorce decree should also require the mother to provide the father with an accounting of the actual expenses incurred. He must be able to prove that child support payments have been made. The mother should also be required to prove that she paid the day-care expenses.

Escalator Clauses

The amount of child support ordered in the divorce decree will be in effect for a long period of time. During this period, the father's income may increase substantially. The amount of the child support obligation, however, does not increase automatically. The mother must go back into court and attempt to get the divorce decree modified. This requires time and money.

In order to assist mothers, it is becoming increasingly common to put escalator clauses in divorce decrees. This is nothing more than a way to adjust child support payments upward without the necessity of the mother going back to court.

There are two basic types of escalator clauses. The first is a periodic increase in the amount of the child support that the father must pay. Sometimes it is just a number pulled out of the air. For example, a father may be required to pay $200 per month to be increased by $20 per month each year. The first year the father would pay $200 per month. The second year he would pay $220 per month, and so on.

Sometimes the periodic addition is based on an economic index rather than a flat dollar amount. One of the most common is the consumer price index (CPI). The CPI measures the rise in the cost of purchasing goods. The father's child support obligation is then increased by the amount of the increase in the CPI.

These periodic escalator clauses do not take into consideration the father's actual income, or his circumstances. They assume that a father will receive an automatic pay increase every year and that he can afford to pay more child support. In reality, a father may have lost his job or have taken a pay cut. Yet, this type of escalator clause would require him to pay more.

The second type of escalator clause is based upon actual raises in income where the father must pay a portion of any increase as child support. For example, a father may be required to pay $200 per month, plus twenty percent of any salary increase. If the father's income goes up by $100 per month, his payment would be increased by $20 per month. However, if his income decreases, the father's obligation is not reduced.

While this type of escalator clause is better than the first one, it does not take the circumstances of the father into consideration. It assumes that he can make an increased payment just because his income has risen. However, he may have remarried and have a new family to support.

If a father's income increases substantially, the children should participate in the increased income. Escalator clauses, however, are not the way to do it. They are a poor attempt to predict what will happen in the future, with little basis in fact. Fathers should oppose having any type of escalator clause written into their divorce decrees.

————————●————————

Variable
Child Support Orders

Once the amount of the child support obligation has been determined, the question arises as to how it is to be paid. Most divorce decrees require the fathers to pay the same amount each week, or month, during the year. Some fathers earn the same amount every month. Some never get laid-off or lose their jobs. For these fathers, it is appropriate that they pay the same amount of child support every month.

For other fathers, earnings and employment are not stable. If a father's income varies, there is no reason why his child support obligation should not vary with his earnings. Many divorce decrees can be written so that the amount of the child support varies with income. These are called variable orders for child support.

PERCENTAGE ORDERS

The most common variable order is a percentage order. It requires the father to pay a certain percentage of his income, rather than a flat dollar amount. It is the fairest of all child support orders for all parties concerned. If a father's income decreases, his ability to pay child support decreases and so does his obligation. Likewise, if a father's income increases, the children participate in the additional earnings.

There are two reasons why variable orders are not as common as fixed-dollar–amount orders. First, the child support enforcement agency does not like variable orders as they are much harder to enforce. The agency must know what a father's income is before it can determine whether or not the father has paid the proper amount. If the father's income is unknown, it is very hard to enforce the child support obligation.

Second, a variable order does not provide the mother a certain sum each month. In order to budget for household expenses, a mother needs to know what to expect in the way of child support. If a father's income varies significantly, the mother will never be able to predict the amount that will be paid.

In order to overcome these problems, many variable orders specify a minimum amount that must be paid regardless of income. For example, the father might be required to pay fifteen percent of his income or $100 per month, whichever is greater. The problem with a minimum, if it is very high, is that it defeats the purpose of the variable order. It becomes nothing more than a child support order with an escalator clause.

In percentage orders, the term "income" needs to be precisely defined. For example, it is gross income or net income? If it is net income, what does that mean? Is a year-end bonus considered income? The wording of a divorce decree must be specific; if there is any doubt, the child support enforcement agency will attempt to interpret the divorce decree in its favor.

EMPLOYED VERSUS UNEMPLOYED ORDER

Under this type of order, the father is required to pay one amount when he is employed and another when he is not. It works well for individuals in the trades, such as ironworkers, who work spordically but know what they will earn when they work. It also suits seasonal employees, such as fishermen and agricultural workers.

Like percentage orders, these attempt to match income with the amount of the child support payment. The payment schedule varies, but is always a fixed dollar amount. As an example, a seasonal worker may be required to pay $200 per month per child while employed, and only $50 per month per child while unemployed. For individuals who work only a part of the year, this arrangement is better than a fixed-dollar order since many fathers do not save enough money to make the child support payments when they become unemployed.

Date of Payment

Regardless of the type of child support order, there should be a specific date when the payments are to begin, and a specific date when the payment is due each month. Many divorce decrees do not specify dates. As an example, an order may require the father to pay $300 per month in child support, and the order may be signed by the judge on May 31. Does the father owe $300 in child support for May? The judge may or may not have intended payment to be made that month. Most likely, he did not even think about it. The child support enforcement agency, however, will probably take the position that the father owes for May.

Based upon the above example, when is the child support payment due in June? Is it due on June 1, June 15, or June 30? It is possible that the father could be required to make a child support payment on May 31, and then be required to make an additional payment on June 1. Or, he could have saved an entire month of child support by just having the dates of payment specified in the divorce decree.

As will be seen in chapter eight, the date on which a child support payment is due is also important when it comes to collection action, which the child support enforcement agency is required to take when a father is one month delinquent in his payments. If the payment date is not specified in the divorce decree, the date when the father becomes delinquent is subject to dispute.

The Age of Majority

The child support obligation usually ceases when the child reaches the age of majority. This is determined by state law and, in most states, is eighteen years of age. But the child support obligation can end before then. Likewise, the judge can order the child support obligation to extend past that age.

Children can become emancipated before reaching legal age if they become self-supporting and self-sufficient. Examples would be a child joining the armed forces or getting married. A divorce decree should specify that the child support obligation ends if the child becomes emancipated prior to the age of majority. If it does not, the father may have to continue to make child support payments until the child reaches legal age.

Usually, child support orders require the father to pay after the age of eighteen if the child has a serious medical problem, or needs it for educational purposes. The most common provision is that support will continue until the child finishes high school. Some divorce decrees require child support to continue through college.

A father should fight any attempt to have child support ordered after the age of majority for the purpose of sending a child to college. Such an order would be imposing a greater responsibility upon the father than he had during the marriage: married couples do not have the legal responsibility to pay for a child's college education. It is absurd that a divorced father should be ordered to pay just because he happens to be divorced.

This is not to say that the father should not pay for a child's college education; he just should not be ordered by a judge to do so. When a father is ordered to pay for college, he loses his rights. He does not have the privilege of participating in the decisions regarding the school, subjects that the child takes, or the grades that must be maintained.

If a father pays for college voluntarily, he has a right to participate in all the decisions relating to his child's educational future. This is better for both the father and his child.

Child Support Payment Records

As stated previously, the burden is on the father to prove that he has made his child support payments; his former wife does not have responsibility of proving that her ex-husband did not pay. Therefore, adequate records are essential. The penalty for not doing so is severe: having to pay a second time.

This problem can be solved by placing the burden of record keeping on someone else. That someone can be either the clerk of the court or the child support enforcement agency. Every divorce decree should include a provision requiring payments to be made through either of these.

The father has the right to have child support payments made through one of these agencies, even if it is not specified in the divorce decree. Federal law requires each state to process child support payments through one of these agencies at the request of either parent. There may be a fee for this service, but it is limited to $25 per year.

CHAPTER 6

———————◆———————

Living with the Divorce Decree

Now that the divorce is final, a father may think that he is free at last. Not quite. When children are involved, there is really no such thing as a final divorce. The relationship between the father, the mother, and the children continues. The difference is that this relationship is now specified by order of the court, and the terms and conditions of the divorce decree specify the rights and responsibilities of the parties.

It is important that the father comply with these terms and conditions exactly as written. This is how the child support enforcement agency will enforce the decree. Many fathers have gotten into trouble because they did not do so. They lived up to the spirit of the decree, but not the wording.

Most of the problems that arise relate to child support and visitation because these are the terms that are in effect for the longest period of time. Circumstances of the parents can change, but the terms of the divorce decree do not. Trouble then begins.

●

Agreements Between the Parties

A divorce decree is an order of the court. For this reason, the terms and conditions contained in it cannot usually be changed by the parents. They must go back to court and have the decree modified. It costs time and money to get a divorce decree changed. Therefore, parents will often enter into an agreement to alter the terms of their decree rather than go back to court. In most states, agreements between the parents to change the child support obligation are worthless. It doesn't matter whether they are verbal or in writing. These agreements do not usually change either parent's responsibility to live up to the terms of the original order.

Assume that a divorce decree requires a father to pay $300 per month in child support. Assume further, that the mother obtains a very high-paying job after the divorce, and that the father loses his position. In order to help him out, the mother agrees to reduce the child support payment to $200 per month. There may never be a problem if both parents abide by this agreement and the child support agency does not become involved.

What if the mother changes her mind a year later and demands the original $300 per month, plus the $1,200 dollars that the father had not paid? The father must now make a monthly child support payment that he cannot afford, as well as come up with past-due money.

If the mother goes on public assistance, the agreement will be ignored and the father will be required to pay according to the terms of the divorce decree. Since all due child support belongs to the state, the enforcement agency is not going to pay any attention to an agreement between the parents that reduces the state's right to money.

If a father's circumstances change, especially as they relate to child support, the divorce decree must be modified. Trying to save money by entering into some type of agreement is just asking for trouble. Don't take the risk.

Payment of Child Support

One of the most common mistakes divorced fathers make is not strictly complying with the terms of the divorce decree relating to their payments. If he does not pay exactly as the decree requires, he may not get credit for the payments he has made.

It is important to emphasize "may not." No one can make an absolute statement as to whether or not a father will get credit for payments that are not made in strict compliance with the divorce decree. Laws vary from state to state. Within a state, it is not always possible to predict what will happen. It depends upon the circumstances of the case, and even the mood of the judge.

What can be said is that a father takes a needless risk every time he does not strictly comply with the payment provisions. The risk is even greater when the mother and children are receiving public assistance because the money belongs to the state. The child support enforcement agency is in business to collect money. It will interpret the terms and conditions of the divorce decree in its favor.

If a father does not agree with the enforcement agency, he can always go to court, and he may win. The child support enforcement agency knows from experience, however, that many fathers will not go to court as most cannot afford it. The father must live up to the *wording* of his decree.

CHILD SUPPORT IS A DOLLAR AMOUNT

A divorce decree will specify that a certain dollar amount be paid each month for the support of the children. That means that a specific payment must be made in dollars on the date required. It sounds simple, yet all too many fathers make the mistake of not following this direction.

Because the mother is the custodial parent, child support is paid to her. She is then responsible for using monies for the care and maintenance of the children. Sometimes, the money isn't used for the children. Their mother may spend it on herself, neglecting to buy the necessities for her children.

In situations such as this, fathers will often buy food and clothing for the children rather than pay the support. The divorce decree, however, requires the father to pay a certain dollar amount and it does not specify that food and clothing can be substituted. If a father does so, he is taking a risk that he will not get credit for making child support payments.

If the mother is neglecting the children, the father should attempt to solve the problem. This may even involve going to court to gain custody. Buying food and clothing for the children, instead of paying child support, is not a solution. At best, it is nothing more than a stopgap measure.

CHILD SUPPORT IS FOR THE CHILDREN

It is not uncommon for the mother to request the father to buy her a car, or some other item, and make the loan payments instead of paying child support. This most often happens when the mother has a poor credit rating. Situations such as this can be risky.

It is the responsibility of the father to make child support payments to the mother. If he makes loan payments, instead of paying his obligation, he may still owe the child support. The mother has a lot of discretion on how she spends the money. She may choose to make loan payments with the child support. The father does not have this choice: he must pay child support.

A father may get credit for paying off a loan if the mother is willing to state that the father was actually paying his child support. What happens if the mother does not do so? It becomes less likely that a father will get credit. She has the opportunity to get paid twice, the mother has the incentive to not make such a statement. Don't take the risk.

A father will have even bigger problems if the mother and children begin receiving public assistance. After notice, a father is required to make his child support payments directly to the child support enforcement agency. He can no longer get credit for making the loan payments. If the loan is in the father's name, he must continue to make the payments. And he must also pay the child support enforcement agency.

ADVANCE PAYMENT OF CHILD SUPPORT

There are certain occupations where the entire year's income is made in just a few months. In those cases a father may want to pay the whole year's child support, in advance, when the money is in hand. It is possible that the father could be required to pay over again because he did not pay the specified amount on the specified dates. More than likely, a father will ultimately get credit for such payments, but he may have to go to court and prove that the payment was for child support.

More importantly, a father cannot be assured that the mother will act responsibly with his money. The mother has the freedom to spend child support monies as she chooses. A father has little control other than the timing of his payments. If he pays a substantial amount in advance, the mother may be tempted to spend it on something she always wanted but could never afford.

A father who wishes to make advance payment should make arrangements with a third party to hold the money. This can be a bank or even the child support enforcement agency. The father pays the entire amount in advance, and child support payments are made by the third party to the mother on the dates specified in the divorce decree. A father is then assured of getting credit for his payments without any hassle. He is also assured that the mother will not spend the money immediately, leaving the children to go without their due for the rest of the year.

OFFSETTING CHILD SUPPORT AGAINST MONEY OWED TO THE FATHER

Sometimes, in the property settlement, the mother will be required to make payments to the father. Situations such as this commonly occur when the mother is awarded the family home in a divorce settlement. She is then obligated to make monthly payments to the father to purchase his equity in the property.

The child support payment, and the payment owed the father by the mother, are two separate issues. If the mother does not pay the father, the father cannot reduce his child support payment by the amount of the missed payment. He must take legal action against her to get his money. She is in violation of the terms and conditions of the divorce decree. This, however, does not change the responsibility of the father to make the full amount of the child support payment.

PAYMENT TO THE CHILD SUPPORT AGENCY

It is worth restating at this point that, if the mother is receiving welfare, the child support belongs to the state. Once a father receives notice requiring him to make payments to the child support enforcement agency, he must do so. It does not matter what the divorce decree states. If a father does not do so, he may have to pay a second time.

Child Support Payment Receipts

As stated throughout this book, adequate records are essential. A father must be able to prove that he paid child support.

The mother does not have to prove that the father did not pay. Thousands upon thousands of fathers have to make double payments every year because they did not keep adequate records. They faithfully paid, but they can't prove it.

The best way for a father to prove that he made his payments is to have them paid through the child support enforcement agency, or the clerk of the court (see chapter five). If a father chooses to maintain his own records, he must be very careful to ensure that they actually prove that he made his payments.

One of the best records is a canceled personal check. The personal check should be in the exact amount of the child support payment. If the check is for more, or less, there is a chance that a dispute could arise as to whether or not the check was really for its designated purpose. And while a check in the proper amount does not prove that it was for child support it is enough to put the burden on the mother to prove that the father did not pay. The personal check should also specify that it is "Child support, month of _____." (This wording does not prove that the check was for child support. A check could be written for something else and the above wording added after the canceled check is received back from the bank. It is, however, another indicator that the father did pay child support.)

Money orders and cashier's checks are not as good as personal checks as there is no copy to keep. All that is on hand is a receipt for the purchase of a money order or cashier's check. These receipts are not proof that the father made his child support payment. To do that, the father must obtain photocopies from the bank, and they are only retained by them for a certain period of time.

Cash is the worst of all possible methods of paying child support. There is no way for a father to prove that he paid his child support obligation, unless the mother provides the father with a receipt. Even then, these receipts are suspect. It is not uncommon for the mother and father to get together and produce fake receipts to defraud the child support enforcement agency. Some fathers force the mother to produce fake receipts under threats of violence. Some mothers will allege that the father forced her to prepare fake receipts, even though the father faithfully paid his child support. Paying in cash presents a needless risk.

Visitation

Fathers must strictly comply with the visitation rights awarded in their divorce decree. If fathers keep the children longer than allowed, they are in violation of the decree. Repeated offenses can result in the loss of the rights to visitation.

If a father takes the children without the mother's permission, he may become a criminal. Many of the missing children on milk cartons and grocery sacks are missing because the father has taken them. This is a crime called parental kidnapping. The punishment is jail, and possibly the loss of visitation rights forever.

In the past, authorities did not like to become involved in domestic-relations issues such as these. Times have changed. The child support enforcement agency is now required by federal law to use its locate resources to track down fathers in parental kidnapping cases. Law enforcement agencies are also expending much more effort to get the children back and punish the father.

Any father who is considering taking his children and

running better think twice. There is much more to lose than
there is to gain. If a father has a visitation problem, he must
attempt to solve it. Parental kidnapping is never a solution.

FATHERS' RIGHTS TO VISITATION

Mothers have the same responsibility as fathers to comply
with the terms and conditions of divorce decrees. They must
allow fathers their rights to visitation. There is no governmental organization, however, to track down mothers and
force them to give fathers these rights. Most child support
enforcement agencies will not even release the addresses of
children to their fathers. They are on their own.

Withholding child support is not usually the solution to
the problem. In most states, visitation and child support are
treated as separate issues. The nonpayment of child support
does not give the mother the right to withhold visitation rights
from the father. Likewise, the father cannot withhold payment of child support if a mother does not allow the father
visitation.

In order to enforce visitation rights, a father may have to
hire an attorney and take the mother to court. However,
courts have a problem when it comes to enforcing a father's
rights to visitation. There is not much that can be done other
than putting the mother in jail. And if the mother goes to jail,
there is no one to care for the children. It is not surprising
that most judges are very reluctant to do this.

A father who is persistent may win but a long and
expensive process will ensue. He may have to take the mother
into court several times before a judge will actually take a

punitive action. He may also have to face allegations by the mother that he is unfit to see the children.

Fathers who cannot obtain their rights to visitation through the system must do it in spite of the system. Legal or not, fathers do withhold child support in an attempt to get mothers to allow visitation. It can be effective, and it is much less expensive than hiring an attorney and going to court. Fathers must remember, however, that it is a bluff; sooner or later, they are going to have to pay the child support. If the child support enforcement agency becomes involved, it will be sooner.

There are fathers' rights organizations that will help a father obtain his rights to visitation. One of the leaders in this area is United Fathers of America. Appendix B contains a listing of the names and addresses of fathers' rights organizations.

---●---

Bankruptcy

Many debts are dischargeable in bankruptcy, i.e., that they are no longer owed. For all intents and purposes, child support is not one of them. A father must continue his monthly child support payments regardless of any bankruptcy action.

In addition, in most instances, any past-due child support that may be owed cannot be discharged in bankruptcy. However, the federal statutes regarding bankruptcy are very complex and the different forms of it can affect how past-due child support must be repaid. This is best left up to a lawyer who specializes in bankruptcy.

Fathers must assume that bankruptcy will not be of any help when it comes to child support. If the child support obligation is to be reduced, it must be done through the courts.

—————●—————

Adoption

On occasion, a father will give up his rights entirely. The mother will remarry and the father will agree to have the children adopted by the stepfather. Once the adoption is final, the father no longer has an obligation to pay child support.

Sometimes the adoption never becomes finalized. The father signs all the appropriate documents and assumes that he no longer owes child support, but the adoption order is never finalized by the court.

This can be a disaster for the father. Years later, his former wife may go on public assistance. The father learns that the adoption was never finalized. He may then be held liable for all those years in which he did not make payments.

In an adoption proceeding, a father should never consider himself relieved of his child support obligation until he has the final court order in hand.

Modification of the Divorce Decree

Many fathers do not attempt to have the divorce decree modified when their circumstances change. Consider the father with a good-paying job when he gets divorced who is ordered to pay a large amount of child support. Later, he loses his job and is forced to take a job paying much less. Because he can no longer afford to make his child support payment, he quits doing so.

The situation worsens each month. When the child support enforcement agency becomes involved, it does not care about the father's financial circumstances. It must enforce the divorce decree.

A father still has the opportunity to go to court, but it takes time to get a divorce decree modified. Remember, though, the court can only modify the child support obligation with respect to future payments. The old debt is still due.

A father may be able to avoid problems such as these if he immediately takes steps to have his child support obligation modified when his circumstances change. Again, it is important to emphasize the word "may." There are no guarantees. The modification process is far from perfect, as will be discussed in detail in chapter twelve. A father may not be successful in getting his child support obligation reduced but it is worth the effort of trying.

THE MODIFICATION PROCESS

Parents cannot go to court for every little change; the courts could not possibly handle the workload. All states, therefore, have developed laws that limit the rights of parents to modify the divorce decree. Most commonly, these laws require there be a "material change in circumstances" before a divorce decree can be modified.

The term "material change" is not very specific, but the concept is easy to understand. There must be a substantial change in one of the parents' circumstances before a court will consider modification of the divorce decree. If a father's income was reduced from $5,000 per month to $4,500 per month, a court would probably not consider it a material change in circumstances. If a father's income were reduced from $1,000 per month to $500 per month, it would most certainly be deemed a material change.

The actual process for modifying a divorce decree is much the same as obtaining the original divorce decree. One parent petitions the court for a modification, and the other parent is served notice of this petition. The parent receiving notice must file an objection within the time period stipulated in the notice.

If a parent objects upon receiving the notice, there will be a hearing, and the judge will make a decision based on the facts of the case. If the parent does not object to the notice, it is a default, and the judge will most likely order the divorce decree modified as requested by the petitioning party.

The traditional modification process is one of the biggest weaknesses of the system. It cannot adequately deal with the needs of the parents. Parents' circumstances can change frequently, but it usually takes months for a modification to be approved by the court. It is also expensive because the parents must acquire the services of attorneys, which many parents cannot afford.

Some states have attempted to simplify the process as it relates to the child support. It is kind of a "do it yourself" modification process. The parents fill out a series of forms. The judge reviews them and makes a determination as to what the new child support obligation should be.

In theory, this type of process is quicker because a court hearing is not required. It is also less expensive because the parents can do it themselves. In reality, a simplified modification process has yet to be perfected in any state. Fathers should be very careful before they attempt to have their divorce decree modified without the services of an attorney.

Most modification actions are contested. The mother does not usually take kindly to the idea of the father trying to have his child support obligation reduced. Likewise, most fathers are not in favor of having their child support obligation increased. Who wants to have their future determined by filling in the blanks on a bunch of forms?

More importantly, an action to modify one of the terms of a divorce decree may open up all terms for possible modification. As an example, one parent may petition the court to have the child support obligation increased. The other parent may ask the court for a change in custody or visitation.

Modification of a divorce decree is not a simple process. A father who tries to do it himself may run into problems that he never considered. Unless both parents are in complete agreement as to the modification, a father should hire an attorney. It costs more in the beginning, but it can save many problems in the future.

It is usually easier for a mother to have the child support obligation increased than it is for the father to have it decreased. Again, there must be a material change in circumstances, usually meaning that a father's income has increased.

How does the mother know when the father's income increases? The father usually tells her. He wants to show the mother how well he is doing and what a big mistake she made in getting a divorce. Fathers are too often guilty of bragging, and it may cost them in the end.

If a father's income increases significantly, his children should participate in the increased income. This does not mean that the child support order should be modified. The child support obligation stated in the divorce decree is nothing more than a minimum that the father must pay under the law. He can always pay as much as he wants; he can never pay less.

CHAPTER 7

━━━━━●━━━━━

Establishment of Paternity

In cases where a child is born out of wedlock, there is an extra step in the process of establishing a child support obligation. The father/child relationship must be legally determined before an obligation can be ordered. The process of legally determining the father of a child born out of wedlock is called the establishment of paternity.

In today's society, with all of the sexual education and availability of contraceptives, one would assume that the number of children born out of wedlock would be decreasing. Sadly, this is not the case. There are more children born out of wedlock today than ever before. Almost one in every five children born in the United States has no legal father.

The child support enforcement agency is required to attempt to establish paternity in all welfare cases and it is also required to establish paternity in non-welfare cases, if the mother requests the service. Most child support enforcement agencies will do nothing, however, to help a father in his efforts. It can be expected that this will change in the next few years. The federal government has recently directed states to begin assisting fathers in establishing paternity.

Child support enforcement agencies have become involved in a big way. There are over 3.5 million cases nationwide, and paternity is established in 270,000 cases each year. In some urban areas, the illegitimacy rate among welfare mothers is fifty percent. This means that one-half of the women receiving welfare in these areas have an illegitimate child. In order to collect child support in these cases, paternity must first be established.

Paternity establishment aids the state, and it can also benefit the child, who will know the identity of his or her father and will possibly be given the father's last name. The child will also have rights to support, to inheritance from the father, and other benefits such as social security.

There are also disadvantages. The process of establishing paternity creates a lifetime relationship among the father, mother, and child. In some cases, the parties involved may not want such a relationship. It can also be a very humiliating experience, and many parents do not want to go through the ordeal. For many mothers, the disadvantages outweigh the advantages, and they do not want to have paternity established. Very few mothers request the child support enforcement agency to assist them in establishing paternity. (Nationally, over eighty percent of the paternity cases are initiated on behalf of mothers who are receiving welfare.)

Paternity and the Father

If a man is a father, he has the responsibility of supporting his child. The circumstances surrounding the pregnancy of the mother are irrelevant in almost every jurisdiction. While a man can be tricked or deceived into getting a woman pregnant, he is still responsible for the outcome. The reasoning is that the child should not suffer just because one of the parents did something wrong.

The woman may have the right to have an abortion without the father's consent. The father, however, does not have the right to require the woman to abort the child. As unfair as it might seem, the mother can do as she wishes and the father cannot do anything about it, except to support the child.

There is no statute of limitations to protect a father. Federal law requires each state to establish paternity until the child reaches the age of majority. It is entirely possible for a man to become involved in a paternity action ten years after the fact for a child he did not even know existed.

One man was fifty-nine years old, and planning for an early retirement, when the child support enforcement agency caught up with him. Many years before, he had been involved with a woman who was twenty-five years younger than he was. The relationship lasted long enough for the woman to become pregnant, and have a daughter. The parents then went their separate ways.

Several years later, the mother lost her job and applied for public assistance. The child support enforcement agency became involved, and an action to establish paternity was initiated on behalf of the daughter, who was then thirteen years old. Paternity was established, and the father was required to make monthly child support payments. He was also required to pay over $10,000 in child support for prior years. This man will be lucky to pay off his debt by the time he is seventy years old.

In this case, money is the issue because of the age of the father. In other cases, however, money is not the most important result of a paternity suit; an action of this kind can destroy a family. One day, a happily married man receives notice in the mail that a paternity action is being initiated against him. Later, his marriage ends in divorce. And a man does not necessarily have to be guilty, the accusation itself can cause marital problems.

Pregnancy is caused by the lack of proper precautionary measures. Pregnancy can also be caused intentionally. A woman may use it to get a husband. She assumes, frequently incorrectly, that the father will marry her if she becomes pregnant.

Not all women want to get married. Some women want to have a child, but do not want husbands. A woman will find a man who she feels is the right person to father her child and get pregnant. Afterward, she ends the affair, without informing the father of the pregnancy.

An argument can be made that it is up to a woman whether or not she wants to have a child in this manner. It is a weak argument because the woman deceived the man into becoming a father. The man has a child and the child has a father, but neither know the identity of each other. If the child support enforcement agency becomes involved, the father will still be required to pay. It does not matter whether or not he knew of the pregnancy.

The best protection against having a paternity suit initiated is not to let it happen in the first place. A man should always take his own precautions since a woman may want to get pregnant for her own reasons, which may not include the father. Every child support enforcement agency has thousands of cases to prove it.

———————————●———————————

Proving a Man is the Father

In the past it was very difficult to actually determine whether or not a man was the biological father of a child. A judge listened to testimony of both parties and made a decision. If the testimony of the parties conflicted, a judge had little upon which to base his decision. The most convincing evidence may have been that the child "looked" like the man accused of being the father.

Today, the process of establishing paternity is much more precise. Laws have been enacted, and scientific tools developed, to assist in the paternity-establishment process. The most powerful of these are the presumptions of paternity and blood testing.

PRESUMPTIONS OF PATERNITY

States have enacted laws to shift the burden of proof to the man in certain circumstances. Those instances in which the burden of proof are shifted to the man are called presumptions of paternity; the man is "presumed" to be the father. In a sense, he is the father unless he takes an action to prove that he is not.

The presumptions of paternity vary somewhat from state

to state. In order to provide an overview, the presumptions of paternity in Washington State are used as an example. In Washington, there are five presumptions of paternity, or five instances in which a man is presumed to be the father, as follows:

1. He and the child's natural mother are or have been married to each other and the child is born during the marriage, or within three hundred days after the marriage is terminated.

2. Before the child's birth, he and the child's natural mother have attempted to marry each other by a marriage solemnized in apparent compliance with law, although the attempted marriage is or could be declared invalid, and the child is born within three hundred days after the termination of cohabitation.

3. After the child's birth, he and the child's natural mother have married, or attempted to marry, each other by a marriage solemnized in apparent compliance with law, although the attempted marriage is or could be declared invalid, and

(a) he has acknowledged his paternity of the child in writing filed with the registrar of vital statistics, or with his consent, he is named as the child's father on the child's birth certificate; or

(b) he is obligated to support the child under a written voluntary promise or by court order.

4. While the child is under the age of majority, he receives the child into his home and openly holds out the child as his child.

5. He acknowledges his paternity of the child in a writing filed with the registrar of vital statistics,

who shall promptly inform the mother of the filing
of the acknowledgment, and she does not dispute
the acknowledgment within a reasonable time after
being informed thereof.

The point to remember is that presumptions of paternity
are very powerful: they place the burden on the man to prove
that he is not the father.

A presumed father may be ordered to pay child support,
even though paternity has not been legally established. As a
matter of fact, most fathers are only "presumed fathers" under
the law. A man will get married and have children. Later, he
may get a divorce and pay child support. There is never any
legal determination of paternity. He is just a presumed father.

BLOOD TESTING

Blood testing has made the paternity-establishment process
much more precise. Through blood testing, it can be scientif-
ically determined with a very high degree of probability
whether or not the man in question is the biological father of
the child.

Children inherit many genetic characteristics from their
parents. Each of these inherited characteristics is controlled
by two genes. A child inherits one gene from the mother and
the other from the father. In a very simplistic sense, if the
mother does not have one of the genes found in the child, it
must come from the father. If a man does not have this gene,
he cannot be the father.

If a man has the gene, he may be the father; there are

many of these characteristics and it is quite possible for any man to genetically match on some characteristics. It is unlikely, however, that a man who is not the father of the child will match on a great number of them.

Certain components of the blood carry these genetic characteristics. By examining the blood of the mother, the child, and the man alleged to be the father, it is possible to determine the probability of paternity with a great deal of precision. The more characteristics that match, the higher the probability that the alleged father is the biological father.

There are several different types of blood tests that can be conducted. One of the most widely used is the human leukocyte antigen (HLA) test. This involves testing the antigens that are attached to the surface of the white blood cells. If a man is not the father, there is a very high probability, ninety-five percent or higher, that the HLA test, in combination with some other blood tests, will exclude him. Likewise, these tests can result in a positive probability, exceeding ninety-five percent, that an individual is the biological father.

A blood test may result in a ninety-nine percent probability that an individual is the father. There is still one chance out of one hundred that he is not. Therefore, there must also be some other evidence, in addition to the blood test, to establish paternity. This other evidence may consist of things such as the man living with the mother, the man having sex with the mother at the time the pregnancy occurred, and so on. If a man is also a presumed father, there is little doubt that the judge will find him to be the father.

Blood tests are costly, approximately $500. If a man is ever involved in a paternity action, these tests can be worth every penny. Blood testing can quickly exclude a man from being the biological father, ending the paternity action. Further, if a man thinks that he could be the father, but is not sure, these tests can help remove any doubt in his mind.

The Process
of Establishing
Paternity

In most states, paternity is established through the courts.
The paternity-establishment process can take only a few days
if an alleged father admits paternity, or more than a year if a
court action is necessary. It may even involve a trial. As will
be seen in this chapter, the alleged father has a great deal of
control over the process of establishing paternity.

With the advent of blood testing, proving that a man is
the biological father of a child has become much easier. The
difficult part of the process is finding out who the possible
fathers are, and then negotiating the terms and conditions of
the order. These are not easy tasks for the child support
enforcement agency.

INTERVIEW WITH THE MOTHER

The process of establishing paternity begins with an interview
with the mother. The purpose of this interview is to determine if she can identify the father, and if there are enough
facts to proceed with the case. If the mother cannot, or will
not, identify him, the child support enforcement agency does

not have a case. A large percentage of cases are closed at this point.

As stated previously, many mothers do not want to have paternity established. They also do not want their welfare grant reduced for not cooperating with the child support enforcement agency. During the interview, some mothers will name the man, or men, who could be the father. Many others will lie. A mother may say that she does not know who the father is, or may name many men who could potentially be the father. She may even name a man that she would like to be the father.

The problem is so bad that some jurisdictions use polygraph machines to try to determine if the mother is telling the truth. The child support enforcement agency does not want to expend time and effort tracking down the wrong man. It also does not want to wrongly accuse an innocent man, because of the problems that it can cause. Even then, innocent men do get hurt.

If the mother does name a man as the possible father, she is required to complete an affidavit attesting to the fact. By completing the affidavit, the mother is swearing under oath that the named man could be the father of her child.

INTERVIEW WITH THE ALLEGED FATHER(S)

The child support enforcement agency will attempt to locate and interview each of the men named as possible fathers. At this point the agency does yet not know if it has a case. It has only heard the mother's side of the story. This interview allows the alleged father to tell his side of the story, and assists the agency in making a decision whether or not to proceed with the action.

This interview also determines the direction that the paternity action will take. If the alleged father admits that the child is his, all that may be necessary is for him to sign some documents. These documents can be processed through the court system and paternity will be established.

If the alleged father is unsure, the agency will gladly arrange to have blood tests conducted. A father does not have to agree to blood testing at this point; court order is required to force a father to submit to blood testing.

If the alleged father denies paternity and can convince the child support enforcement agency that he is not the father, the case will be closed. If not, he will be served with legal notice. The formal process of establishing paternity then begins.

This interview should be approached with caution. The primary objective is to get the alleged father to admit to paternity and sign the appropriate documents. An alleged father should not agree to anything at this point, even if he is certain that he is the father. There are several other issues which must first be resolved, such as child support and visitation. An alleged father who agrees to paternity, without these other issues being resolved, loses much of his bargaining power.

NOTICE

The formal legal process to establish paternity begins with a notice. This notice is called a summons and petition to establish paternity, complaint to establish paternity, or something similar. It is served by personal service or by certified mail. Often it is served during the initial interview with the alleged father. This notice informs a man that he has been named as the father of a child in a paternity action, and that he has a duty to support the child.

As with all other notices, there will be a certain time period in which the alleged father must respond. If he does not answer within the required time period, paternity may be established by default. As stressed throughout this book, a default is usually the worst possible thing that can happen. In the case of a paternity action, it can result in the wrong person being legally determined to be the father. Once an order has been entered, it is usually difficult to get it overturned.

Some jurisdictions serve this notice on the alleged father before he is interviewed by the child support enforcement agency. The primary reason for this is that many men will not voluntarily come in for an interview. This notice forces them to do so. There is no consistent practice regarding the time at which the notice is served, even within states.

TRIAL

If the alleged father and the child support enforcement agency cannot come to an agreement, the case goes to trial. Evidence is presented and a decision is made. Because the court system is overburdened, it may be months, or even a year, before the trial can take place, and only a small percentage of paternity actions actually go to trial. Most actions are settled through a negotiation process. The establishment of paternity is the most expensive and time-consuming activity that the child support enforcement agency must perform. There are extensive staff expenses. There are also blood test charges, filing fees, court costs, and maybe even the price of a jury trial. This can add up to thousands of dollars on a single case, and states just cannot afford to incur these costs on the large volume of cases that they must handle.

Additionally, most paternity suits are initiated on behalf of recipients of welfare who do not want paternity established. They cooperate only because the law requires them to do so. If a mother terminates welfare she no longer has to cooperate. The child support enforcement agency may then have to drop the case; the longer the paternity action takes, the more likely this is to happen.

The alleged father has a geat deal of bargaining power. He is in a position to control the time, effort, and costs that the child support enforcement agency must incur before the paternity suit can be resolved. The child support enforcement agency knows this, and will usually try to settle the case as quickly as possible.

---•---

Negotiating with the Child Support Enforcement Agency

The first priority of a man alleged to be a father is to determine as conclusively as possible whether or not he is really the biological father. This means that, if there is any doubt whatsoever, a blood test should be conducted.

Since blood tests are expensive the agency will want the alleged father to pay for their cost. An alleged father should not consent to a blood test unless the child support enforcement agency agrees that it will pay for it. If the alleged father does not consent to the test, the child support enforcement agency will be forced, sooner or later, to petition the court to order to have it done and the court will often order the child support enforcement agency to pay for the blood tests.

The alleged father may be ordered to reimburse the agency for the expense of the blood test, if he is found to be the father. Most likely, repayment will be on an installment basis. In the best case, the father will be able to negotiate his way out of any cost by settling the suit prior to trial.

Once the blood tests are conducted, the results of the tests may exclude the alleged father, in which case the paternity suit is over. Alternatively, the tests may show a high probability that the alleged father is the biological father. These tests are not one hundred percent conclusive. If the alleged father still feels that he is not the biological father, he must fight. Child support is not the only issue: the establishment of paternity involves the establishment of a lifetime relationship.

Once the alleged father is convinced that he is the biological father, he must try to negotiate the best deal that he can. There are six issues that must be addressed in the paternity action:

> **1. *The monthly child support obligation.*** Other than the establishment of paternity, the monthly child support obligation is the primary concern of the agency. Most jurisdictions will negotiate the monthly obligation within limits but a father should not expect to obtain a child support order more

than a few percentage points below the established
schedule. He can have greater success in negotiating
some of the other issues, such as past-due child
support.

2. The amount of past-due support. A father
must know that he can be held liable for child
support prior to the date in which paternity was
established. There is usually a limitation on the
number of years in which child support can be
assessed retroactively. The length of time varies
from state to state, but it can be five years or more.
    The amount of past-due child support is nego-
tiable. The larger the amount, the more negotiable
it is. In most instances, it is better to negotiate on
past-due child support than on the monthly child
support obligation since a child support order is
always subject to modification. A father might receive a reduced child support order initially, but
there is nothing to prevent that order from being
modified upward at a later time.

3. Birth costs. A father may be held liable for
some or all of the birth costs of the child, which are
almost always subject to negotiation, especially if
several years have passed since the child was born.
Accurate records of the actual birth costs may not
even be available.

4. The costs of the paternity action. Most child
support enforcement agencies are very reluctant to
negotiate on the costs of the action, such as blood
tests, and will seek reimbursement from the
"proven" father. These agencies have their own
operating budget out of which they may have to pay

these expenses. If the agency is not reimbursed, it loses money. The child support enforcement agency is out for the good of the cause, but charity begins at home.

5. Visitation. A father desiring visitation rights must introduce his wishes into the negotiation process. If it is not addressed, or only mentioned with a meaningless phrase, another legal action will have to be initiated to gain these rights. An uphill battle can result. Many times, the mother will not want the father to have anything to do with the child.

A paternity suit is very emotional time for a father. He may be confronted with a child that he never knew was his. He often feels that everything that is happening to him is the child's fault. As a result, he wants nothing to do with the child and does not even consider issues such as visitation. This is usually a mistake. As the years pass, the father's attitude can change and he may want the child to become a part of his life.

6. The child's last name. This issue may be more important to some fathers than others. If it is, he should request that his child's name be changed. If he is required to pay child support, he should have the right to have the child carry his last name.

The primary rule in the negotiation process is to ensure that all issues are addressed at the same time. The alleged father's bargaining power exists because of the problems the child support enforcement agency has in establishing paternity. If the issue of paternity is separated from the other points, the alleged father will lose most of his bargaining power. It is for this very reason that child support enforcement agencies attempt to isolate the issue of paternity from these other issues. Don't let it happen to you.

CHAPTER 8

Enforcement of Child Support Obligations

Jack had been divorced for several years, but he remained very close to his children. He visited them every other weekend and always made his $400 child support payment on time. It wasn't easy; Jack was now remarried and had a second family to support. He managed, but never had any money left over at the end of the month.

The company that Jack worked for was facing hard times because of foreign competition. In order to keep his company in business, the union was in the process of making certain concessions to management. One of these concessions was a temporary salary reduction. Everyone would feel the impact, but it was going to be especially hard on Jack. He had no money to spare, and would not be able to pay all of his bills.

In order to preserve his credit, Jack contacted all of his creditors and attempted to negotiate a reduced payment schedule until his salary was restored to normal. He also contacted the child support enforcement agency and attempted to have his child support temporarily reduced. Jack was told it was not possible; he must make the payment. There are no excuses.

Jack continued to make his child support payments, but instead of paying $400, he paid only $250. It was all he could afford. Nothing happened for the first two months, but in the third month, he received a notice stating that his wages were being garnished. Sure enough, the child support enforcement agency took half of his next paycheck.

The child support enforcement agency locates fathers and establishes child support obligations. Its primary business, however, is to collect child support and each year, the agencies get better at it. Collections have more than doubled in the last five years. Today, $4 billion a year in child support is being collected.

The increase in collections is due, in part, to the fact that child support agencies are becoming involved in more separation and divorce cases each year. More important to the father, however, is the fact that new and more ruthless ways of collecting child support have been developed.

In the past, the court system was the primary mechanism for enforcement. A father who did not make his child support payments was taken to court where the judge would give him a choice; begin paying or go to jail.

The court system never really worked very well for collecting child support because it was a slow and expensive procedure. Further, it was not realistic to put fathers in jail; there simply was not enough space. States, therefore, began to look for other ways to enforce child support obligations. The result was a series of new and powerful laws which allow the agency to go directly against a father's assets without the necessity of court action.

As will be seen, the enforcement agency has many different collection means. Its success, however, depends greatly upon its ability to locate a father's assets. This is why it is so important to fully understand the locate sources available to the enforcement agency (see chapter three). A father cannot always avoid having collection action taken against him but he can be aware of what to expect.

---●---

Obligations Enforced by the Child Support Enforcement Agency

The term child support is very misleading when it comes to enforcement. More and more enforcement agencies are becoming involved in seeing that most of the terms and conditions of a divorce decree are met, except for those relating to custody, visitation, and the property settlement. The "child support" that is collected is almost everything that the father owes the mother. Depending upon state laws, and the terms of the divorce decree, the child support enforcement agency may collect some, or all, of the following:

1. The monthly child support obligation
2. Past-due child support
3. Alimony, or spousal maintenance
4. Medical support ordered in the divorce decree, or other medical expenses the father is required to pay
5. Day-care expenses the father is ordered to pay

6. Interest on past-due child support
7. Attorney fees and/or the costs incurred by the child support enforcement agency in collecting from the father.

Most agencies will not enforce these other obligations unless there is also a monthly child support obligation involved. For example, the child support enforcement agency will probably not collect alimony for an ex-wife if there are no children.

Additionally, many child support agencies will not collect past-due money owed to the mother after the children are emancipated; if the child support enforcement agency was not involved in collecting prior to the children reaching the age of majority, it probably will not take the case. If the money is owed to the state, however, a father can be sure that the child support enforcement agency will come after him.

The objective of the child support enforcement program is to collect money for the state or for children. If there is no current monthly child support obligation owing, neither the state nor the children benefit. The money goes to the mother.

Wage Withholding Requirements

Wage withholding has become the primary enforcement mechanism used in the collection of child support. Through wage withholding, the child support enforcement agency can go directly against a father's wages without the necessity of court action. If a father does not pay his child support, and the child support enforcement agency knows where he works, his earnings can simply be taken.

The wage withholding process is very similar in every state because there are strict federal requirements that must be followed. The terminology varies from state to state. It may be called wage garnishment, withholding, attachment or assignment, payroll deduction, or order to withhold and deliver.

PROVISION FOR WAGE WITHHOLDING IN CHILD SUPPORT ORDERS

All new child support orders issued must now contain a provision for wage withholding as a means of enforcing the commitment. This includes both temporary orders and divorce decrees. The wage withholding provision must be added to older child support orders if they are modified. In most states, though, it is not actually necessary that this wording be in that order. Agencies have enacted laws to allow the attachment of wages whether or not the wording is in the order.

This requirement is important to remember, however. First of all it allows a mother to initiate a withholding action without going through the child support enforcement agency. Second, some states have added the words, "without further notice" to the wage withholding provision of the child support order. By doing so, action can be taken without advance notice against a father who becomes delinquent in his child support obligation.

TRIGGERING WAGE WITHHOLDING

Wage withholding must be implemented if the father is delinquent in an amount equal to one month of child support (thirty days). This means that, if one monthly child support payment is missed, the agency is required to implement wage withholding. In this case it does not help to make partial payments. If the father has made every one, but not in the proper amount, it must still be implemented when the total amount that is past-due equals one month of child support.

The thirty-day requirement is a maximum. States can use any other time period as long as it does not exceed the thirty-day federal requirement. As an example, Washington State has enacted legislation which allows wage withholding when a father is only fifteen days delinquent. The state of Wisconsin has immediate wage withholding; a father does not have to be delinquent at all.

Congress has recently enacted legislation that would require all states to implement wage withholding immediately upon establishment of the child support order. It is incorporated in the national welfare reform bill (the Family Support Act), which was discussed in chapter one. Welfare reform costs money. The immediate wage withholding provision is an attempt, in part, to make fathers pay the bill.

As currently written, this legislation would only apply to new child support orders established, or modified, after January 1, 1994 (January 1, 1991, for temporary orders that are established by the child support enforcement agency). Additionally, the parents have the right to "opt out" for some other type of payment mechanism if they so choose.

It is also not known how many states would actually implement immediate wage withholding regardless of what Congress mandates. Congress, itself, is not sure that it is the right thing to do, and has directed that a study be conducted to determine the implications of immediate wage withholding. The year 1994 is a long time away, and many things can happen between now and then.

AMOUNT OF WAGES TO BE WITHHELD

Federal law requires that the amount of pay withheld be sufficient to meet the monthly obligation, plus a portion of the amount in which the father is delinquent. For instance, if the current monthly obligation is $300 per month, $300 must be withheld, plus an additional amount to go toward paying off the past debt.

The maximum amount that the enforcement agency can take is controlled by the Consumer Credit Protection Act. Up to sixty percent of a father's net income can be taken if he has not remarried. If he has remarried, the maximum is reduced to fifty percent. These percentages can be increased to sixty-five and fifty-five percent respectively if the father is more than twelve weeks delinquent in his child support payments.

TERMINATION OF WAGE WITHHOLDING

Once wage withholding is implemented, it does not necessarily stop when the father has paid his past-due child support.

It is binding until notice is given to the employer. Even if a father completely catches up, wage withholding may continue.

Some states will terminate wage withholding after a father has paid his past-due support, and has regularly made his monthly payments for a period of time. Other states will never release the wage withholding order. Under these circumstances, a father must change jobs to get out of wage withholding. Even then, if the new employer is located, the state may again implement wage withholding. The trend, nationally, is to leave wage withholding in place once it is implemented.

PRIORITY OF WAGE WITHHOLDING

Wage withholding for child support takes priority over all other legal processes against a father's wages, except for deductions required by law (federal income tax, social security, mandatory retirement benefits, and so on). Child support is withheld next. Any other deductions, such as a credit union payments, are taken only after the child support obligation has been satisfied.

Assume that a father's net monthly income, after taxes, is $2,000. Assume further that there is a $500 credit union deduction for a car payment. If the child support enforcement agency were to withhold fifty percent of the father's net income, the credit union deduction would not be taken into consideration. The agency would take fifty percent of the $2,000 net income, or $1,000. From the remaining $1,000, the credit union would take its $500, and the final paycheck would only be $500.

EMPLOYER LIABILITY

An employer must implement wage withholding. Failure to do so will result in the business becoming liable for the amount of child support that would have otherwise been withheld from the worker's pay. This potential liability forces employers to comply.

EMPLOYER FEES

Wage withholding does involve a cost for the employer. Many states permit the employer to deduct a fee for the costs incurred, in addition to the child support payment. This means that the father may be required to pay a fee for having his wages withheld. Usually, the fee is minimal, not more than a dollar or two per paycheck.

———————●———————

Implementing Wage Withholding

What the child support enforcement agency is required to do under federal law, and what it actually does, are two different things. Mandatory wage withholding simply cannot be executed each time a father is thirty days delinquent.

First, the father must be employed. If he is self-employed, works for cash under the table, or is unemployed, there are no wages to be withheld. There are other collection tools (see chapter nine) that may be used in these cases, but wage withholding is not one of them.

Second, the enforcement agency must know where the father works. Wage withholding is not automatic. Someone must tell the employer to withhold wages, and how much to take. There are hundreds of thousands of employers in any given state.

Third, the father usually must reside in the state that is attempting to enforce the child support obligation. A state's authority to take a father's wages does not cross state lines. There is an exception to this rule when the father's employer also does business in the state that is enforcing the child support obligation. Because the employer does business in both states, the child support enforcement agency may be able to require the employer to withhold a father's wages.

Lastly, the father must have a stable job with one employer. Each time a job change is made, the enforcement agency must locate the new employer and initiate a new wage withholding action. By the time a new employer is located, the father may have moved on to another job.

Assuming all of the above criteria are met, the process is very simple. The father is given a notice informing him that his wages will be taken, and the employer is notified to begin withholding wages.

NOTICE TO THE FATHER

A father must be provided with advance notice before the first collection action can be taken. This notice is usually sent by certified mail, or served personally. It is called a notice of financial responsibility, notice of debt, notice of wage withholding, or something similar.

As discussed previously, a few states have enacted laws whereby the notice is contained in the child support order. In those cases, language is added stating that collection may be taken without further notice if the father becomes delinquent.

In the majority of cases, however, the father receives a notice that indicates that collection action may be taken, and it is not necessarily limited to wage withholding. Most likely the agency can take any type of collection action after the notice has been served. It usually contains the following information:

1. Notification that the child support enforcement agency is involved in the case

2. Notification that all child support payments must be made through the child support enforcement agency, or the father will not get credit for them

3. The amount of the current monthly child support obligation, as specified in the divorce decree or other order for support, and the amount of overdue child support that is being claimed

4. The procedures for contesting the amount of the debt, and the time period in which a father is required to respond to the notice.

In some states, a father may be given notice every time a collection action is taken against him. In others, a father need only be given notice once; collection action can be taken from then on. It is safest for a father to assume that all of his assets are fair game after the receipt of any notice.

The notice is usually the first step in the collection process. It does not necessarily mean that the support agency will take action, or that it knows where a father is employed or his assets are located. The notice merely gives the agency the right to take action.

The collection notice is like any other; the father is allowed a certain period of time to contest its validity before action can be taken. (The process of contesting the notice is explained on page 127.)

NOTICE TO THE EMPLOYER

After the father has been provided with advance notice, wage withholding can be implemented simply by providing notice to the employer to withhold wages. It tells how much to deduct from the father's pay, where to send the money, and the penalty for not doing so. Some states mail an informational copy to the father, others do not.

Immediately the employer begins withholding the specified amount from each paycheck and pays it to the child support enforcement agency. Once wage withholding begins, it is continuous. The employer is required to deduct the specified amount from each paycheck until the child support enforcement agency notifies it otherwise.

The wage withholding order may remain in effect for a period of time after a father quits or gets laid off. If a father goes back to work for the same employer, he may have his wages withheld again. A new notice does not have to be issued.

In some occupations, people move from job to job, but work for a particular number of employers and all of them can be served with a wage withholding order. If the father goes to work for any of these employers, he may have his wages withheld.

There is nothing that a father can do to have the employer change the amount withheld, even if it is wrong. The only way to get the amount changed is to contact the agency; a new order for the correct amount will be issued.

Fathers should carefully monitor the amount deducted from their checks each pay period. Employers most often make mistakes when employees are paid biweekly. Assume, for example, that a father owes $200 per month in child support and that he is paid every two weeks. Many employers will program their computer to deduct $100 from each paycheck, for a total of $200 per month. The problem is that there are three paychecks in some months. The father would have $300 deducted from his paycheck in those months, with the result of an overpayment of $100.

Wage Withholding and the Father

Obviously, the best strategy for a father is to never become delinquent in his obligation. In real life, however, there are times in almost every divorced father's life when he cannot afford to make the payment.

If only one payment is missed, it is possible that wage withholding could be implemented. Once a payment is missed, he may not be able to avoid it, even if the past debt is paid off. Under federal law, wage withholding must start if a father has become thirty days delinquent. The fact that a father paid his past-due child support debt does not change this requirement. Remember: once a payment has been missed, the child support agency is going to ensure that it does not happen again. Do keep in mind, however, that it is nothing more than a payroll deduction, which is becoming a very common way of paying for things. But don't forget that it can also be a disaster. A father must therefore negotiate a deal that he can live with, or he will be forced to run.

There are three primary issues to be concerned with relative to wage withholding. The first is to ensure that the amount stated in the notice is correct. The second is to determine whether or not the amount being withheld is reasonable. The third is to stop the agency from taking other collection actions against the father.

CONTESTING THE AMOUNT OF THE DEBT

The amount of the monthly obligation and the sum of past-due support stated in the notice are the totals that the agency is attempting to collect. It is imperative that these amounts be correct. In every state, a father has a right to contest the amount stated in the notice, which should contain information explaining the procedures for contesting. In most instances, it is just an informal hearing and a father can represent himself but the burden of proof is on the father. The enforcement agency does not have to prove that payment was not made.

Some fathers are reluctant to contest the debt for fear the agency will find out where they are employed. This is a mistake. A father does not have to reveal his employer in order to challenge the charges.

THE AMOUNT OF INCOME TO BE WITHHELD

The child support enforcement agency probably does not know how much the father is earning, or can afford to pay. Therefore, it is a very common practice to require the employer to withhold the maximum amount allowed by law. This can be as much as sixty-five percent of net income, before voluntary deductions. If a father has a number of voluntary deductions, he can end up owing more each pay period than he earns.

After one or two paychecks are taken, an irate father usually contacts the child support enforcement agency. A deal is then negotiated for a more reasonable amount. A new order is then sent to the employer, who begins deducting a lesser amount.

This procedure works well for the agency, but it is very hard on the father. By the time a new order is in place, the father has had a great deal of money taken from several paychecks, which can cause a severe financial hardship. And it is highly unlikely that the agency will give any of the money back.

This situation can be avoided. A father who is employed, and plans to remain at the same job, should contact the child support enforcement agency immediately upon receipt of the notice. This provides an opportunity to negotiate a reasonable payment before wage withholding begins.

In the negotiation process, a father must remember that he is required to pay his monthly child support obligation, plus something on the past-due support. The agency cannot accept less than the monthly obligation but it has a great deal of freedom to negotiate on the amount of the past-due support that the father will be required to pay each month.

MULTIPLE COLLECTION ACTIONS

The child support enforcement agency is in the business of collecting money, and it can be ruthless. As will be seen in the next chapter, there are many enforcement actions, in addition to wage withholding, that can be taken against a father. Several enforcement actions can even be effected simultaneously. If a father makes a deal with the agency regarding wage withholding, it does not necessarily mean that other enforcement actions will not be taken to collect child support owed. It is imperative, therefore, that any deal made specify, in writing, exactly what other enforcement actions will or will not be taken.

Past-due child support is due and owing immediately. Any agreement, even a written one, is probably not legally enforceable, and child support enforcement agencies do break their agreements. Therefore, when this happens, a father may not get any help from the courts. If the agreement is in writing, however, a father can often use the governmental complaint process to force the child support enforcement agency to live up to it, legal or not. (This process will be explained in chapter eleven.)

---●---

Statute of Limitations

If a father avoids paying child support for a certain period of time, he no longer owes it. The time period is governed by a law called a statute of limitations. Each state has its own statute of limitations, and almost every state is different.

As an example, Washington State has a ten-year statute of limitations on child support obligations. If any part of the debt is more than ten years old, it is no longer owed. The entire debt is not forgiven—only that portion which is older than ten years.

In order to understand the statute of limitations, think of each month's child support obligation as a separate debt. If a father has a child support order requiring him to pay $100 per month and he misses twenty payments, $2,000 is owed. That amount is composed of twenty separate debts of $100 each. If any one of those debts is older than the time period specified by the statute of limitations, the father is no longer responsible for it.

Every father who owes past-due child support should become familiar with the laws regarding the statute of limitations in his state. Enforcement agencies do not always take into consideration the statute of limitations when calculating a debt, and the burden is on the father to raise the issue.

The statute of limitations can also be important in negotiating the amount of wages to be withheld. The agency has the authority to set any repayment amount on the past-due child support. However, it does not want to make the payment so low that child support is lost due to the statute of limitations. Often, a father cannot afford to pay an amount sufficient to avoid the statute of limitations problems.

The problem may be solved by the father signing a waiver of the statute of limitations, thereby giving up his right to have his child support obligation forgiven due to the statute of limitations. In return, the child support enforcement agency accepts a lower monthly payment on the past-due amount.

———————•———————

Termination of Employment due to Wage Withholding

In the past, many men have been fired as a result of income withholding. There are now legal protections to prevent this from occurring. The federal Social Security Act now requires each state to have laws subjecting an employer to penalties for firing, taking disciplinary action, or refusing to employ an individual because of income withholding. The law in the state of Washington reads as follows:

No employer shall discharge or discipline an employee or refuse to hire a person for reason that an assignment of earnings has been presented in settlement of a support debt or that a support lien or order to withhold and deliver has been served against said employee's earnings. If an employer discharges or disciplines an employee or refuses to hire a person in violation of this section, the employee or person shall have a cause of action against the employer. The employer shall be liable for double the amount of lost wages and any other damages suffered as a result of the violation and for costs and reasonable attorney fees, and shall be subject to a civil penalty of not more than two thousand five hundred dollars for each violation. The employer may also be ordered to hire, rehire, or reinstate the aggrieved individual.

Every state has a law similar to this. It is extremely important that every divorced father be aware of the law in his state. It can save his job.

CHAPTER 9

Enforcement of Child Support Obligations: Other Collection Practices

Wage withholding is the primary collection mechanism used by child support enforcement agencies, but it only works in a portion of the cases. Less than thirty percent of monies collected are derived through wage withholding. There are a whole series of other collection tools. Once a father has been provided notice, as discussed in the previous chapter, he must assume that any, or all, of these other collection actions can be taken against him.

It happened to Tom. He was a dairy farmer, a self-employed businessman, who was used to making a lot of money. However, times had been tough for the last couple of years. Tom could no longer afford to maintain the life-style to which he was accustomed. Something had to go, and he decided that it was going to be his $1,000 a month child support payment.

Tom had two children from his previous marriage, and had been divorced for a number of years. He was not close to his children, and seldom visited them. The relationship between him and his former wife could only be described as bad, especially since she remarried a man who Tom considered to be a bum. Tom felt that he was sacrificing his life-style to support his former wife and her new husband. It was time to stop.

Things went well for a long period of time. Occasionally, Tom would receive a notice from the child support enforcement agency directing him to withhold his own wages for child support. He merely threw them away. He figured that anyone stupid enough to withhold his own wages deserved what he got.

One day, however, Tom received a notice from his bank stating that he was $5,000 overdrawn. The child support enforcement agency had taken all of the money out of his business checking account. Tom became irate, but he knew that there was nothing that he could do about it. They beat him once, but it would not happen again.

Sometime later, Tom's truck driver reported that the distributor to which he delivered milk would not pay him. He immediately telephoned the distributor and was told that the child support enforcement agency had taken the money. Tom informed the distributor that he would never do business with the company again.

Tom found other distributors, but the same thing happened. The child support enforcement agency had arranged it so that he could no longer sell his milk. Tom was down and broke, but he was not defeated. He decided to borrow some money on the farm to tide him over until this "thing" went away. The bank that he had done business with for years, however, would not loan the money. The child support enforcement agency had placed a lien on his property.

In Tom's case, he got what he deserved. If a father can pay child support, and will not, he is fair game. However, some child support enforcement agencies do not always use these collection tools responsibly. They abuse their power by taking action against fathers who are paying child support.

Since the entire amount of past-due support is owed immediately, the enforcement agency can legally make a deal with a father to pay a certain amount each month, and use another collection remedy to get more money. It does happen, especially as it relates to the income refund tax intercept programs, which will be explained in the next section. The agency can wipe out a father who legitimately cannot afford to make his child support payments just as it can a father who purposefully neglects to pay his obligation.

Every father who is paying support to the best of his ability should take precautions so that multiple collection actions cannot be taken against him. Wage withholding is hard to escape if a father is steadily employed and does not want to quit his job. However, many of the other collection actions can be avoided with a little common sense.

IRS Income Tax Refund Intercept

A father who is delinquent in his child support payments may be certified (reported) to the Internal Revenue Service (IRS) for a federal income tax refund offset. Any income tax refund due the father will then be intercepted and given to the child support enforcement agency. This method of collecting is second only to wage withholding. Almost two million fathers are certified to the IRS each year, and $340 million in income tax refunds are intercepted.

There are some restrictions on certifying cases to the IRS for income tax refund offset, but they are minimal:

1. There must be an order requiring the father to pay child support.
2. If the mother and children are receiving public assistance, the amount of past-due child support must be at least $150, and the debt must be at least three months old.
3. The amount owed must be at least $500 if the mother and children are not receiving public assistance.

THE IRS CERTIFICATION PROCESS

The process is automated, and extremely simple. The child support enforcement agency sends a computer tape containing fathers' names, social security numbers, and past-due child support debts. If an income tax refund is due any of these fathers, the amount of the debt is deducted from the refund and sent to the agency. The remaining portion of the refund, if any, is then sent to the father.

The IRS certification process begins in the fall of the year before the actual offset will occur when the agency sends a computer tape of fathers who are delinquent in their child support obligation to the IRS. The IRS then matches the computer tape against their files. When a match occurs, the IRS file is flagged for income tax refund intercept.

The next step in the certification process is to notify the father. This is called a pre-offset notice, and it is mailed before the end of the year. It informs the father that his case has been certified to the IRS. It also states the amount of past-due support being certified, and advises the father of his right to contest the action.

The pre-offset notice is prepared by either the state child support enforcement agency or the IRS. Usually, it is prepared by the latter. The address to which it is sent is the one on the most recent income tax return. There is a major difference with the notice requirement for the IRS intercept and the one required under wage withholding: the father does not actually have to receive the pre-offset notice. Many fathers have their income tax refund intercepted without ever receiving advance notice.

When an income tax refund is actually intercepted, the IRS will send an offset notice to the father, informing him that his refund has been forwarded to the child support enforcement agency. Again, there is no requirement that the father actually receive this notice. Most fathers do, however. It is sent to the address to which the income tax refund was to be mailed.

CONTESTING THE ACTION

A father does not have the right to contest the interception itself. He does, however, have the right to argue that the debt is incorrect, or that he is not the right person. The IRS is not involved in this process; it must be done through the child support enforcement agency.

The initial notice contains the information necessary for contesting the action. Usually it is nothing more than an informal administrative review, which does not require the father to hire the services of an attorney. Staff of the child support enforcement agency review the case, plus any evidence that the father might have, and make a decision.

The certification process is automated, but mistakes are often made. A father must ensure that the debt is correct because the records of the child support enforcement agency are not always accurate. A father must also make sure that he is the right person. Computer matches are based upon name and social security number. One incorrect digit in a social security number may result in the wrong person being certified to the IRS.

In one case, the income tax refund of a seventy-year-old man, who had never been involved with the child support enforcement agency, was intercepted because of a transposed digit in a social security number. A father with a similar name was certified to the IRS, but his social security number was recorded incorrectly. The incorrect social security number matched that of the seventy-year-old man.

In another case, a father was using a false social security number. His name, and what was thought to be his real social security number, were certified to the IRS. It just so happened that the "phony" social security number actually belonged to someone else with a very similar name. The other man's income tax refund was intercepted, and it was not all that easy for him to prove that he was the wrong man because he lived in another state.

Fathers who wish to contest either of these issues should do so as soon as they receive a pre-offset notice. The child support enforcement agency has a process to decertify cases from the income tax refund offset, and this process does take time. The longer fathers wait, the less likely it will be that their cases will be decertified in time to avoid having their income tax refunds intercepted.

If a father is not decertified from the IRS intercept in

time, the income tax refund will go to the child support
enforcement agency, which in turn is responsible for reim-
bursing the father.

JOINT RETURNS

If a man has remarried, he will probably have filed a joint
income tax return. A portion of any refund due belongs both
to him and his new wife. And while the part belonging to her
cannot be taken to pay the father's child support obligation,
the IRS will intercept the entire amount of the refund. There
is no advance mechanism to separate the amount due the
father from that due the new wife.

In order to obtain the wife's share of the refund, it is
necessary to file an amended return, Form 1040-X. The offset
notice, provided by the IRS, contains information regarding
the procedures to follow. The child support enforcement
agency is not involved in this process. Any money due will be
paid to the new wife by the IRS, and the agency must then
repay the IRS.

DISTRIBUTION OF MONIES COLLECTED

The IRS income tax refund intercept program was not developed to help mothers or children. It was developed as a means

to help government get back some of the money that it has spent. Any monies collected are first applied to government debts. These debts are not just for child support. If there is anything left over, it is given to the mother and children.

There is a priority sequence involved in which any monies collected must be applied. The first priority is the repayment of public assistance. If the mother and children have received welfare, and there is still a debt owing, the monies are first applied to that debt.

Monies collected this way are distributed differently than other child support collections as they are applied only to past-due child support. All other types of child support collections must first be applied to the current monthly support obligation, and then to past-due child support. This means that the mother and children do not receive the first $50 of the payment (see chapter two).

If there is no public assistance debt, or the income tax refund is greater than the debt, any monies intercepted must be applied to government-insured defaulted student college loans. This relates to instances where individuals borrowed money for college and did not repay the loan. It has nothing to do with the child support enforcement program directly, other than these debts must be paid before any IRS intercept monies can be given to the mother. The child support enforcement agency is not involved in collecting on defaulted student loans. This is the responsibility of other governmental agencies.

The remainder of the money is given to the mother and the children but the government in fact keeps almost eighty percent of the money that is intercepted. Only a little over twenty percent goes to the family.

AVOIDING THE INCOME TAX REFUND INTERCEPT

Many child support enforcement agencies are doing a wholesale IRS certification. This means that every case that meets the federal requirements for offset is certified to the IRS. It does not matter what kind of agreement the father has with the child support enforcement agency, or how much he is paying.

If a father is not trying to pay his child support obligation, intercepting an income tax return is fair game. However, it is an abuse of power on the part of the child support enforcement agency to take an income tax return from a father who is paying according to an agreement. In cases such as these he can choose not to get an income tax refund.

An employer deducts income tax based upon information contained on a W-4 form, which is completed by the employee. If a father normally gets a refund, he can complete a new Form W-4, claiming more exemptions. A smaller amount of income tax will then be taken from each paycheck, his take-home pay will be increased, and he will not receive an income tax refund. This way there is nothing for the child support enforcement agency to intercept.

ILLEGAL INCOME TAX DEDUCTIONS

Beginning with the 1987 tax returns, child support enforcement agencies started to help the IRS to find fathers who are "cheating" on their income tax. The records of the child support enforcement agency are used to help identify fathers who do not pay child support, but claim the children as dependents on their income tax returns.

All taxpayers are now required to include the social security number of their dependents, age five or older, on their income tax returns. The social security numbers of children who are being claimed as dependents will be matched against the social security numbers of children receiving welfare. When a match occurs, the IRS will then check with the child support enforcement agency to see if a father has been paying his debt. If a father has not been paying his child support, the deductions claimed for his children on the income tax return may be disallowed.

Beware: an income tax refund can be intercepted by the child support enforcement agency; yet, the IRS can require repayment for incorrectly claiming children as a deduction.

State Income Tax Refund Intercept

States that have an income tax are required to have a state income tax refund intercept program. At the time of the writing of this book, only ten states did *not* have an income tax. Those states are as follows:

Alaska
Connecticut
Florida

Nevada
New Hampshire
South Dakota
Tennessee
Texas
Washington
Wyoming

The intercept process is very similar to the federal program. A computer tape, containing information regarding fathers who are delinquent in their child support obligation, is sent to the state tax department. Any state income tax refund due is intercepted and forwarded to the child support enforcement agency.

The rules and regulations of the state program are also very similar to those of the federal one: A father must be provided advance notice that his state income tax refund will be intercepted. (The child support enforcement agency, however, may not attempt to provide notice each year, as in the federal IRS intercept. The initial notice that the father receives may be all that he gets [see page 123].) A father must also be afforded the right to contest the amount of the past-due child support alleged to be owed. Every state has procedures to give a second wife her share of any refund that may be due under state law.

Each state is allowed to determine the amount of past-due child support that must be owed before a father can be certified for the state income tax refund intercept. The amount is usually less than for the IRS intercept. Some states certify fathers who owe as little as $50 in past-due child support.

If a state has an income tax, it is likely that the child support enforcement agency will attempt to intercept both the federal and the state income tax refunds. The child support enforcement agency will not certify one half of the debt to the state and the other half to the federal government. The entire debt will be certified to both and a father can end up paying much more than he owes. This situation can be partially avoided by not getting a federal income tax refund. Depending upon the structure of the state income tax, it may be harder to avoid getting a state income tax refund.

The state of Alaska is different from others in that it has established a permanent fund from which it makes payments to residents each year. In a sense, this is a tax refund and thus is also subject to the state tax intercept.

---●---

Withholding Unemployment Compensation Benefits

Federal law requires that all states have procedures for withholding unemployment compensation benefits from fathers delinquent in their child support obligations. Federal law also requires that state child support enforcement agencies enter into cooperative agreements with state employment security departments to implement withholding of unemployment compensation benefits.

It is much easier to take unemployment compensation benefits than it is to take wages. There are thousands of employers in every state where a father might be working, but there is only one agency that pays unemployment benefits. Further, many child support enforcement agencies have computer access to the records of the state employment security department. Information regarding unemployment compensation benefits is immediately available.

Withholding of unemployment compensation is required by federal law but many states are reluctant to do so. This is due, in part, to the fact that fathers cannot afford to pay very much child support when they are receiving unemployment compensation benefits. In 1986, twenty-one of the fifty states collected less than $100,000 in child support from unemployment compensation benefits. Four states collected nothing. In 1987, only $37 million in child support was collected from unemployment compensation benefits nationwide.

Based upon federal statistics, the twenty-one states that collected the least from the unemployment compensation intercept in 1987 are as follows*:

Alabama	$ 0
Delaware	55,783
Florida	73,059
Georgia	57,155
Hawaii	29,379
Kentucky	38,306
Massachusetts	0
Mississippi	0
Nevada	75,138
New Hampshire	60
New Mexico	31,060
North Dakota	34,568
Oklahoma	15,195
Rhode Island	18,004
South Carolina	0

*U.S. Department of Health and Human Services, Office of Child Support Enforcement, "Child Support Enforcement, Twelfth Annual Report to Congress," Volume II, Table 13.

South Dakota 37,924
Tennessee 7,168
Vermont 36,274
Virginia 70,645
West Virginia 94,512
Wyoming 48,726

If a father lives in a state that does little to collect unemployment compensation benefits, he has nothing to worry about. If not, there is much more room to negotiate than there is with wage withholding. Under payroll deduction, the child support enforcement agency must withhold the entire amount of the monthly support obligation, plus something on the past-due support. There is no such restriction when it comes to withholding unemployment compensation benefits. The child support enforcement agency may accept as little as a few dollars per month.

If a father's unemployment compensation benefits are intercepted, he should immediately contact the child support enforcement agency and negotiate a reasonable payment. Many fathers, though, are very reluctant to do so. For some reason, they feel that unemployment compensation benefits are a gift, and do nothing when it is taken. This is a big mistake.

●

Seizing Bank Accounts

The most common assets taken by the child support enforcement agency are liquid assets, such as checking and savings accounts. In many states, the agency can go directly after these assets. The process is very similar to wage withholding. Notice is given to the financial institution and any monies held by them must then be turned over to the child support enforcement agency.

An entire savings account may be taken since the agency is not limited to a certain percentage of the money, as it is under wage withholding. In addition, it is quite possible for sixty-five percent of a father's wages to be taken through wage withholding, and the remainder when the father deposits his check in the bank.

This collection remedy can totally wipe out an individual's savings. It is even more harsh when checking accounts are seized. The child support agency can take all the money in the account without considering any outstanding checks that may have been written. A father not only loses the money in his account—all of his outstanding checks will bounce.

It is common for older parents to put their adult children's names on their bank accounts, providing a way for the children to get to the money if something should ever happen to the parent. If the "child" is a divorced father with a child support debt, the agency may take the money from the parent's account. These monies will most often be refunded if adequate proof can be provided showing that the monies belong to the parents. Under no circumstances should the monies of the parent and child be comingled.

When a father remarries and the bank account is a community account, the issue of what the child support enforcement agency can take becomes much more complex. A portion of the account may belong to the new wife. Regardless, the entire account will probably be taken. The burden is then on the father to prove that some of the money belonged to his new wife.

If a large account is actually taken, a father should immediately contact the child support enforcement agency, and probably an attorney, to find out what his wife's rights are. Again, this is a complex issue. It not only depends upon state law; it may also depend upon the source of funds, i.e., that of husband or wife. Additionally, the type of funds may make a difference, such as earnings, opposed to interest income or the proceeds of the sale of community assets. Each case must be decided individually.

In order to take a bank account, the agency must find it. If a father has ever made his child support payment by personal check, the agency probably knows where he banks since records of father's bank account numbers are often maintained. Fathers who pay their obligation by personal check are well advised to keep the monies in that account at a minimum.

This collection remedy should only work once, and only for those individuals who do not know the system. If a father is delinquent and does not have the resources to pay the delinquency, it is best not to keep any more in a checking account than is necessary to make the monthly child support payments.

---●---

Seizure and Sale of Property

Most child support enforcement agencies have the authority to seize personal property, such as boats and automobiles, for child support debts. This authority is used much less frequently than other collection remedies as it is a very expensive process.

First, the property must be physically seized. Once the property is taken, it must be stored. Then the property must be sold. Additionally, the agency becomes liable for any damage that might happen to the property, and there usually isn't enough equity in the possession to make it worthwhile.

When property is seized, it is not usually for the purpose of selling it. Rather, the property is "held hostage" until the father comes up with the money to get it back. A waiting game ensues between the father and the agency. A father who redeems the property will most likely get stuck with the storage bill in addition to child support.

If a father has a $50,000 Porsche, and is not paying child support, he had better keep it well hidden. However, there should not be any fathers with such an expensive automobile who are not paying child support.

———————●———————

State Lottery

Many states are legalizing certain gambling activities as a way to increase revenue. One of the biggest is the state lottery. It is becoming a common practice to offset debts owed to the state against lottery winnings. This not only applies to child support, but also to other debts, such as delinquent taxes.

In one case, an individual won $50,000 per year for twenty years in a state lottery. His first year's winnings were reduced by the amount he owned in past-due support. Additionally, his child support obligation was immediately increased $2,400 per month. After taxes and child support, this poor fellow was lucky to break even.

There is really no way to beat this other than not playing the lottery. More importantly, he will save the money, however small, he would have otherwise spent on lottery tickets.

Property Liens

Liens are very common in the child support enforcement program. Even if a father is paying his commitment faithfully, the enforcement agency will probably place a lien on his property to secure any past-due child support debt. Should the father sell the property, the agency is entitled to the father's equity in the property.

There are two types of property. The first is real property, which consists of the land and the permanent structures attached to it. The second is personal property and covers any item that is not real property, such as automobiles, furniture, and clothes.

Liens can be placed on both real and personal property but agencies are mostly concerned with real property since there is usually more equity in real property than in personal property.

The agency does not have to locate a father's real property to place a lien on it. It can just file a general property lien with the county auditor. Some states have laws that automatically place liens on property for child support obligations. In either case, all property owned by the father in that county becomes subject to the lien. Property purchased after the lien is filed may also become subject to it.

It is possible for the agency to foreclose (take the property from the father and sell it) on liens to satisfy the past-due debt. For the most part, this does not happen as foreclosing is a time-consuming and expensive process. It is much simpler to wait until the property is sold, which provides the father with a distinct advantage. If he does not have to sell the property, he can wait. Depending upon the laws regarding the statute of limitations in the particular state, the child support obligation may be forgiven before the father sells the property, and the lien may have to be released.

If the property is sold, the lienholders are paid in order of the priority of the lien. For example, assume that a father was buying a house through a local bank, and that the agency later placed a lien on the property. The bank is first holder of the lien and the agency is the second.

If the father later sold the house, the proceeds from the sale would first go to the bank to pay off the mortgage with remaining monies applied to the child support lien. The father would not receive any money until both these debts were paid in full.

Often the amount of the child support lien is greater than the father's equity in the property. This effectively prohibits the father from selling the property because the proceeds would not be enough to satisfy the lien. Under these circumstances, the enforcement agency will often reduce the lien so that the property can be sold with the agency taking the proceeds. It will also place a lien on any new property that is acquired.

If a father has his own business, a lien placed on those assets can preclude obtaining credit, and result in the failure of the business. If this should happen, the child support enforcement agency should be contacted immediately: it may be possible to have the lien released.

———————●———————

Credit Bureau Reporting

In the past, child support debts have not been on an equal level with consumer liabilities such as automobile loans and credit card charges. In granting credit, lending agencies did not take into consideration the amount of a father's child support obligation, or his record of payments. Credit was extended based upon the amount of outstanding consumer loans and the record of payments on those loans.

Federal law now requires the child support enforcement agency to provide credit bureaus with information on fathers who have a past-due child support debt in excess of $1,000 if the bureau requests it. Only a few states are actually supplying this information. In the future it can be expected that child support debts will become a part of all credit reports.

This is a passive enforcement remedy. It does not force a father to pay his child support but it does make it much more difficult for a father to get credit if he does not do so.

———————●———————

Self-Employed Individuals

People who work for themselves have two distinct advantages over individuals who are employed by others. First, wage withholding does not work. Few self-employed individuals will honor a wage withholding order against themselves. Second, self-employed individuals have the opportunity to hide many of their personal assets in the business or corporation.

Remember though that the child support enforcement agency can take action against the self-employed father's business. As explained in the previous chapter, the employer (business) can be held liable for any child support that was not properly withheld from the employees' wages; the agency can issue a wage withholding order against a self-employed father. If the order is not honored, the business itself then becomes liable for the child support debt. Once this happens, the enforcement agency can then go after the assets of the business, using most of the collection practices contained in this chapter.

This method of collecting child support is not done on a large scale as it is very labor intensive and can become quite complex. A father who has a lucrative business, however, and does not pay his child support, must consider the assets of his business to be at some risk.

———————●———————

Contempt of Court

Years ago, contempt of court was one of the most widely used enforcement remedies in the collection of child support. Today it is used much less frequently because more powerful collection tools are available, such as wage withholding. It is usually used as last resort, when everything else fails.

The contempt of court process operates under the threat of punishment. If a father has a court order requiring him to pay child support and he does not do so, he can be held in contempt of court for not complying with the terms of the order. In other words, he disobeyed an order of the court. If found in contempt of court, the father can then be thrown in jail.

Very few contempt actions result in the father actually going to jail, but it does happen. Most often, the judge will order the father to begin paying the current support, plus a certain amount on the past-due child support, as a condition of staying out of jail.

The most important thing to remember about the contempt process is that the order entered by the judge usually only keeps the father from going to jail. It does not reduce the collectibility of the debt. The entire child support debt is still due and owing.

As an example, assume that a father has a child support order requiring him to pay $300 per month current support, and that he is $2,000 behind in his payments. Assume further that the judge finds him in contempt of court, and orders him to pay the current charges of $300 plus $100 per month on the debt until it is paid in full.

If the father faithfully complies with the judge's order and pays the $400 per month, he keeps himself out of jail, but that is all. The child support enforcement agency is not prohibited from taking additional collection action against him.

———————————●———————————

Other Collection Techniques

Some states have undertaken activities called "round-up day," or "most wanted lists." Under the round-up–day concept, the child support enforcement agency will pick a certain day, such as Father's Day or Christmas, and attempt to arrest several fathers for nonpayment of child support. The most wanted list involves publishing the names, and child support debts, of a few fathers in a newspaper and asking for information regarding their whereabouts. Usually, there is also a warrant issued for their arrest.

The state of Texas was one of the first to undertake such activities. Some of the other states that have done so are Alabama, Indiana, Missouri, and Wisconsin. A father can expect that all states will try things such as this from time to time. However, no state has a comprehensive program to do so. It is more of a publicity stunt than anything else. It creates press for the child support enforcement agency, but doesn't collect much child support. A father's odds of becoming involved in one of these activities are better than the odds of winning the lottery, but not by much.

CHAPTER 10

─────────●─────────

Interstate Child Support Enforcement

The interstate enforcement of child support obligations refers to cases in which the mother and children physically reside in a different state than the father. Our society is highly mobile, and it is becoming increasingly common for one of the parents to move to another state after separation or divorce. In these cases, the rules of the game change.

When a father moves out of state, the child support enforcement agency loses much of its power. A state must have legal authority (jurisdiction) before it can take action against a father. For the most part, the authority of a state to take action does not cross state lines.

Some states have enacted laws called "long-arm" statutes. These laws attempt to give a state jurisdiction to establish a child support obligation against the father, under certain circumstances, even though he no longer resides in that state. As an example, a paternity law may specify that a person who has had sexual intercourse in a state submit to the jurisdiction of that state in an action brought to establish paternity. Even though a father moves to another state, the courts of the state where he had sexual intercourse may still establish a child support obligation. Even so, the court does not have the right to take a father's property in another state, other than as explained later in this chapter.

Long-arm statutes are used infrequently. In most instances, the state in which the mother and children reside must request the state in which the father lives to take action. There are almost 700,000 such requests each year. If, however, a father receives a notice that another state is attempting to establish a child support obligation against him, he should consult an attorney immediately.

From a father's perspective, the procedures for establishing and enforcing a child support obligation in an interstate case are very similar to those where both parents live in the same state. A different state is just doing the work. From the standpoint of the child support enforcement agency, the process is very different. It is much more difficult to establish and enforce child support obligations across state lines.

First, the enforcement agency must know which state to ask for help. As explained in chapter three, it is much more difficult to locate a father when he moves since states do not have the same access to each other's records as they do their own. A father who moves frequently may never be found.

Second, the state in which the father resides must take action. Child support enforcement agencies do not like to work cases for other states. It costs money, and any child support collected goes back to the other state. Child support enforcement agencies are not adequately staffed to handle their own caseload, much less those of other states. Most states, therefore, place a higher priority on their own cases.

Third, there is a communication problem. A state must have certain information to take an action against a father. As circumstances of the mother and the children change, new information must be provided. The information exchange process among the states is poor. It may take months for a state to get the necessary information required to take an action.

The information flow problem is complicated by bureaucracy. Every state has slightly different procedures and forms that must be completed. If a form is not filled out exactly as a state wants it, the case may be sent back to the originating state. This can happen several times on a single case. The interstate child support enforcement process has never worked well and is the biggest single problem that child support enforcement agencies have today.

●

The Interstate Enforcement Process

One of the obvious problems in interstate child support enforcement is distance. The mother and father may live hundreds or even thousands of miles apart. It is not economically feasible to travel to the state in which the father resides every time some type of action is needed.

The interstate child support enforcement process was developed, in part, to eliminate the necessity of travel. It is a document process. The state where the mother resides provides the state where the father lives with enough written information so that action can be taken.

There are two different procedures that a state can use in the interstate child support enforcement process. The first is called the Uniform Reciprocal Enforcement of Support Act (URESA Act). This is the most comprehensive procedure.

Child support obligations can be established; paternity can be determined. All of the available state procedures for enforcing child support obligations can be used under this process.

The second procedure is for wage withholding only, which is a more limited type of action. It is, however, a much quicker process than the URESA Act.

In order to understand the mechanics of the interstate child support enforcement process, one must first become familiar with the following terms:

Initiating State. The initiating state is the one in which the mother and children live. This state "initiates" a request to the state in which the father lives for a child support enforcement action to be taken.

Responding State. The responding state is the one in which the father lives. It "responds" to the request from the initiating state for assistance in collecting child support.

———————●———————

The URESA Act

The Uniform Reciprocal Enforcement of Support Act has, traditionally, been the primary mechanism used for establishing and enforcing child support obligations in interstate cases. All fifty states, the District of Columbia, Guam, Puerto Rico, and the Virgin Islands have adopted some form of the URESA or similar statute.

Mechanically, a petition is filed in the court of the initiating state. The mother, or mother's lawyer, can file the petition. Likewise, the child support enforcement agency can file the petition. The court reviews the petition to verify that the father owes a duty to support and that all the documents are in order. The petition is then forwarded to the appropriate official in the responding state.

ESTABLISHMENT OF THE ORDER

The first step in the URESA process is to establish the child support obligation in the state in which the father now resides. In a sense, the father gets to begin anew. The new child support order may be for much less than the original order. It may also be for more than the original order.

The father will receive a notice stating that he has a responsibility for paying child support, and that he must answer within a period of time or a default will be ordered against him. It will also state the amount being requested for the monthly child support payment and the amount claimed as past-due child support. This notice is very similar to the notice a father would receive from the child support enforcement agency if he resided in the state in which the mother and children lived.

Like most other notices provided by the child support enforcement agency, the father can default, in which case an order will be entered against him without his having the opportunity to defend himself. He can appear at the hearing by himself, or with his attorney to represent him. He can contact the child support enforcement agency to try to negotiate a deal.

The best tactic is to first attempt to negotiate with the child support enforcement agency. Neither the state taking the action, nor citizens of that state, benefit from the efforts put forth. Some other state does. Therefore, if time and money can be saved by making a deal, the responding state will usually do so.

Additionally, the responding state is working only from documents that the initiating state provided. There is often concern on the part of the responding state as to the accuracy of the past-due child support specified in those documents. The father has a great deal of bargaining power as to the amount of past-due debt to be assessed against him. Some jurisdictions are reluctant to order any past-due because of staff limitations and inadequate documentation.

If a satisfactory agreement is negotiated, it is processed through the court system and becomes the child support order. If an agreement cannot be reached, the case is scheduled for a hearing. The judge or hearings officer will then determine the amount of the order.

There are basically two types of orders that are established through the URESA process. The most common is to create a new URESA order. The second is to register the original order with the court of the responding state.

URESA Order

A URESA order usually addresses only the issue of child support, and is a separate order from the original divorce decree. The URESA order sets the amount of child support that the father owes in the new state in which he resides. *It does not change the amount of child support owed under the original divorce decree.* This is extremely important, and is often misunderstood by both fathers and lawyers.

Assume, for example, that a father was divorced in the state of California and ordered to pay $300 per month in child support. Subsequently, he moved to Idaho and a URESA order was entered, requiring him to pay $200 per month. The father only owes $200 per month in the state of Idaho. In California, however, he still owes the original $300 per month. The father also continues to owe any past-due child support that has accrued under the California order. If he ever returns to California, the original order of $300 per month will be enforced, retroactively.

REGISTRATION OF THE ORIGINAL ORDER

As an alternative to establishing a URESA order, the responding state can register the original order with the court. Once the original order has been registered, it becomes enforceable in the new state.

The process of registration usually modifies the order that was established in the initiating state. If a father's child support order is registered in the responding state, and the child support obligation is reduced from $300 per month to $200 per month, that is most likely all the father owes in either state. In other words, the new state modified the original order, and it is binding upon both states.

The process of registration also opens up the possibility

of modifying the other terms and conditions contained in the order, such as custody and visitation. Therefore, many states are reluctant to use the registration process; a URESA order is established instead.

Once an order is established under the URESA process, the responding state can use any of its collection powers to enforce the child support obligation as long as the father continues to live in that state. These actions are the same as those explained in the previous chapters.

If the father moves to another state, all the work that the responding state did is in vain and the case will be closed. The entire process then starts all over again. The child support enforcement agency in the state where the mother lives must locate the father and initiate an action to the state in which the father has moved. The new state in which the father resides must then go through the process of attempting to establish an order and enforce the child support obligation.

---●---

Wage Withholding

States are now required to implement wage withholding based upon a child support order established in another state. This means the state in which the father resides must honor the child support order issued by the state in which the mother resides for purposes of wage withholding. Under the URESA Act, a new child support order must be established, or the original order must be registered with the court.

This does not provide any state with additional power since every state can implement wage withholding through the URESA cases. It merely speeds up the collection process. A considerable amount of time and effort is required to establish an order. By eliminating the necessity to establish another order, the child support agency can take enforcement action much more quickly.

States have a choice. They can request interstate child support enforcement action through the URESA process, or they can request wage withholding. If wage withholding is requested, it is the only action that the responding state is required to take. If wage withholding action cannot be taken for some reason, the case will probably be returned to the initiating state. The initiating state must then make a new request for other types of collection action to be taken under the URESA Act.

The federal government has been placing considerable pressure on states to improve the interstate process. Within the next few years, fathers can expect states to enact statutes to allow them to establish and enforce child support obligations on a more simplified basis. This does not necessarily mean, however, that states will do a better job.

---•---

Actions that can be Taken by the Initiating State

Most of child support enforcement actions taken in interstate cases are initiated by the state in which the father resides. There are, however, certain actions that can be taken by the state in which the mother resides. The most common are IRS income tax refund intercept and, to a lesser extent, wage withholding.

IRS INCOME TAX REFUND INTERCEPT

The IRS intercept is one of the few child support collection actions that can cross state lines. It does not matter where a father resides—he does not even have to live in the United States. Any state in which a father owes a child support obligation can certify the case to the IRS to intercept the father's income tax refund.

The IRS intercept extends across state lines because it is a collection action taken by the federal government. States only provide the necessary information; the federal government does the rest.

It is not uncommon for a father to owe a child support obligation in several states. Many times the mother and children move frequently and have received public assistance in different areas. It is often the case that all of these states would certify the father to the IRS.

If an income tax refund is intercepted, the money is paid to the states on a first come, first serve basis. The state that certified initially is the first to get the money. If there is any left over, the second state that certified gets its share, and so on. For this reason, states race each other every year to be the first to submit their certifications to the IRS.

IRS intercept is also used in cases where a URESA order was established for a lesser amount than the original child support order. The state where the original order was entered will certify the father to the IRS each year for the difference between the two orders. As an example, assume that a father had a child support order for $300 per month. Later he moved to another state and a URESA order was established for $200 per month. The state with the $300 order would certify the father to the IRS each year for the $1,200 difference.

A father is entitled to an administrative review to contest the amount of the debt for each state that certified him to the IRS. A father can request this review by the state(s) that certified him, or by the state in which the order was entered. If a father does not choose to receive a federal income tax refund, however, he doesn't have to worry about contesting the action.

WAGE WITHHOLDING

Under limited circumstances wage withholding can be initiated against a father who resides in another state. The child support enforcement agency may be able to implement wage withholding if the father works for an employer who also does business in the state that is attempting to collect child support. This depends upon state law. It also depends upon the circumstances of the case.

Procedurally, the child support enforcement agency would serve a wage withholding order on a company branch office located within the state. The company is then liable for implementing wage withholding just as if the father were working for the company in the state taking the action.

The child support enforcement agency can also take action to withhold wages for child support from civilian federal and military personnel. Like the IRS intercept, it doesn't matter which state the father resides in. The federal government must honor requests for wage withholding if the documents are in order.

Military personnel are afforded more protection than other fathers. A father who is in the armed forces must be at least two months behind in his child support payments before wage withholding action can be taken. He is also afforded thirty days to provide evidence that the wage withholding notice is in error. If there is a material error in the notice, wage withholding will not be implemented. Other fathers are not given such an opportunity. The employer must implement wage withholding regardless of whether or not the notice is correct.

OTHER ACTIONS

There are some other actions that can be taken by the state in which the mother resides. As an example, it is possible that a father could be extradited from the state in which he resides. This means that he could be brought back forcibly to that state so that action could be taken against him.

Most of these other actions are not practical, and are seldom used. States do send letters threatening all sorts of action. In reality, there is little that a state can do cost effectively on its own other than IRS certification and limited income withholding.

CHAPTER 11

---●---

Protecting
Your Rights

The child support enforcement agency has a tremendous amount of power, matched only by that of the Internal Revenue Service. The agency also has wide discretion in how it uses this power. This can, and does, lead to abuse.

There are two situations in which the child support enforcement agency most commonly abuses its power. The first is taking too much money, up to sixty-five percent of a father's income. There is simply not enough left over for the father to live on, especially if he has a second family.

The second situation is taking multiple enforcement actions against a father who enters into an agreement to pay a certain amount each month. Later, he may find that the child support enforcement agency has taken both his state and federal income tax refunds. It may not be ethical, but it *is* legal, because all past-due child support is owed immediately.

Reasons that Abuse Occurs

On occasion abuse occurs because a child support officer is out to get someone. This is the exception rather than the rule, however. Most of the abuse occurs for one of the following reasons:

The Former Wife. The former wife wants the money owed to her, and she wants it at once. When the money doesn't get to her on time, she complains. Thousands of these telephone calls and letters are received every month. These complaints put considerable pressure on the child support enforcement agency to take harsher actions against the father.

Overzealous Support Enforcement Staff. Support enforcement staff are hired to collect money and their performance rating is very often based upon the amount they amass. Promotions are also based upon employees' success in collecting child support from fathers. The more money that an employee collects, the greater the chance for promotion. The system, therefore, has a built-in incentive for abuse.

Large Caseloads. Most support enforcement staff have such large caseloads that it is not uncommon for one worker to have 1,000 cases or more. With such a heavy workload, it is not possible to give much personal attention to any one case. Therefore, many things are done on a wholesale basis. A good example of this is the certification of cases to the IRS for income tax refund offset. Rather than examining each case, some child support agencies certify all particulars to the IRS.

Regardless of whether a father may have entered into a written agreement that no additional collection will be taken against him he will be certified to the IRS. If the father complains, his money may or may not be returned. If he remains silent, the money is kept. This saves the child support enforcement agency a lot of time, at the father's expense.

--------●--------

Dealing with Abuse

No father has to put up with abuse. There is a very effective system in place to deal with these situations. It is called the government complaint process, and it works. There is a common misconception that complaints to government fall on deaf ears. Everyone has heard the expression, "You can't fight city hall." Nothing could be further from the truth. It is easy to fight "city hall"—and win. Most people fail because they don't know how to do it correctly.

All government agencies ultimately report to an elected official whose goal is to be re-elected. For this to happen, the public must be satisfied. A complaint represents an unsatisfied person and a potential lost vote, so a great deal of time and effort is spent in attempting to resolve complaints and satisfy the voting public. Fathers may not be considered equal when it comes to child support enforcement; all fathers, however, have an equal vote when the time comes to re-elect a public official.

When dealing with government, the one who complains in the right way to the right people is the one who gets the action. This is true for all governmental agencies. It doesn't matter whether an individual is trying to get a building permit or trying to stop abuse on the part of the enforcement agency. The same principles apply. It is extremely important, therefore, that everyone know how to use the complaint process.

Very few fathers understand and use the complaint process to their benefit. Mothers seem to be much better at it than fathers. Their most common complaint is that not enough is being done to collect from the father.

Only about fifteen percent of the complaints are from fathers, and many times they are the injured party. In a real sense, mothers are forcing the child support enforcement agency to take actions that would not have otherwise been taken; fathers are approving of these actions by remaining silent.

---●---

The Complaint Process

When a complaint is made to a particular government official, the response is usually signed by that official. Sometimes, the answer will be signed by yet another official. This occurs when the complaint was made to a very high office such as that of a senator or the president. In these instances, the response will begin with a statement that the complaint has been referred to "the other official" for response.

Regardless of who signs the response to the complaint, it is almost never prepared by that particular official. In government, the employee who took the action is most often the one who actually prepares the response. It does not matter to whom the complaint was directed.

Assume, for example, that a complaint was written to the governor. The governor's office would forward the grievance to the appropriate state agency for a draft response. From there it would filter down to the employee who is responsible for the complaint. This person is then given the assignment of preparing a proposed response for the governor's signature.

Once a draft response is prepared, it is sent back up through the chain of command. Each supervisor compares the statements in the complaint to the draft response. If the employee has adequately justified the action taken, and no relief can be granted, the response will be signed and mailed. If not, the response will be returned, and the employee will be ordered to grant relief.

There is another misconception on the part of the public that, if a complaint is made, the governmental agency will retaliate. This is simply not true. Government and workers alike hate complaints. They make the workers look bad and can result in bad performance evaluations.

Governmental agencies often do keep records of individuals who complain. It is not for purposes of retaliating against these individuals, however; it is usually to be more careful of them in the future. The fact of the matter is that people who complain receive better treatment. The old saying that "the squeaky wheel gets the grease" is very true in government.

●

Designing the Complaint

The most important part of the complaint process is for the
father to take the initiative to act. All fathers become angry
when the child support enforcement agency abuses its power.
Only a small percentage of fathers, though, actually follow
through with a complaint to government.

Once a father has taken the initiative to act, he must
design the complaint properly. There are five essential rules
that must be followed:

> **1. A complaint must focus on discretionary ac-
> tions.** Many complaints fail in this regard, focusing
> on issues over which the child support enforcement
> agency has no discretion. Some of the actions taken
> by the agency are mandatory, and some are discre-
> tionary. For example, the agency is required to
> implement wage withholding if a father is delin-
> quent in his child support obligation. The amount
> of the wages that are withheld, however, is discre-
> tionary.
>
> A complaint can do nothing about a *mandatory*
> action such as wage withholding. It can, however,
> do much to change a *discretionary* decision, such as
> the amount of a father's wages that are being with-
> held. Discretionary actions taken by a government
> employee that cause undue hardship are hard to
> justify. For example, how does an employee justify
> taking sixty-five percent of a father's income, rather
> than fifty-five percent, or forty percent, or thirty-
> five percent? It is impossible to do.

2. A complaint must create a problem. A properly designed complaint must create a problem for the government to solve. This places the burden on the employee to prove to his superiors that the action he took was the right thing to do, which is much different that what is legally correct under the law. The child support enforcement agency does abuse its power, but it does not usually violate the law.

As an example, assume that the agency was taking fifty percent of a father's wages. The father could make a complaint, stating that the agency was wrong to take so much of his wages. This type of complaint does not create a problem that must be solved. The employee who handles the action does not have to prove that his step was the right one. He need only show that he had the legal authority to take fifty percent of that father's wages.

Alternatively, the father could make a complaint that the child support enforcement agency was taking fifty percent of his wages and he cannot afford food for his family. This type of complaint does create a problem. The issue is no longer whether the employee had the legal authority to take the father's wages. The issue now is whether taking fifty percent of the father's wages was the right thing to do.

The employee who took the action must justify to his superiors why so much money is being held. While the employee had legal authority to take the action, it was not the right thing to do. Relief must be granted to the father.

3. A complaint must contain a solution. A complaint must contain a solution to the problem as well as state the relief desired. If it does not contain a resolution, the agency must decide what relief should be granted. The complaint was made because the father did not like the first decision. Chances are, he will not like the second judgment either.

Remember that the solution proposed must be realistic. The sounder the solution, the more likely that the father will obtain the desired relief. The complaint process works well in stopping abuse. However, it will not stop the child support agency from collecting altogether.

4. A complaint must be concise. To be effective, a complaint must be factual and should only contain the necessary information relating to the problem at hand. Too often, complaints contain a whole series of problems. By the time someone is done reading the complaint, he or she does not know the real issue, and the resulting response may be to the wrong problem.

5. A complaint must be polite. Regardless of all else, a complaint must be polite. If the tone is offensive, it will almost automatically be considered invalid. The general feeling will be that the father got what he deserved.

The reverse is also true. If a father states that the enforcement officer was uncooperative and offensive, it may help in obtaining the desired change. Allegations regarding misconduct put the employee in a bad light. Superiors are more likely to think that the employee's action was inappropriate if his conduct was suspect.

Written versus Telephone Complaints

By far, the best complaint is written. It allows the systematic laying out of a problem along with the proposed solution. The person who must prepare the response will have a copy of the letter, and will know exactly what the problem is.

Telephone complaints do not get the attention of their written counterparts. Most telephone grievances do not even make it through to the intended official. Calls are screened, and complaints are routed to someone else, usually a secretary. This person will listen to the complaint and attempt to understand the problem, and then contact the support enforcement officer responsible for the case to find out the facts. The secretary may also make the decision as to what action should be taken.

Too often, telephone complaints are subject to misinterpretation. The person taking the call may not have correctly understood the problem. Even if the person understands the problem at the time of the call, he or she will probably forget some of the facts within an hour or so. If the facts must be given to someone else, they may not be communicated correctly.

The major drawback to the written complaint is the time required; the response to a telephone call is much quicker. When time is of the essence, the only alternative is to use the telephone, but the same care should be taken to properly prepare a telephone complaint just as if it were a written complaint. Additionally, care should be taken not to become emotional. When this happens, the original subject matter of the complaint is often lost.

————————●————————

Directing Complaints to the Proper Official

A complaint must be solvable. It must also be directed to someone who has the power to clear up the problem: the superior of the employee who caused the problem in the first place. Only superiors in the employee's direct chain of command have the authority to overturn a decision made by that employee. Other officials, such as legislators, can only put pressure on the child support enforcement agency.

A father can make a complaint to any official in the chain of command. This begins with the immediate supervisor of the employee who took the action, and ends with the governor. Don't waste time: go directly to the top.

In the complaint process, there are two key officials. The first is the state child support enforcement program director. This is one official in every state who has overall responsibility for administering the child support enforcement program. Since he is the one that looks bad when mistakes are made, many complaints are resolved at this level.

The second is the governor, the chief executive of the state, who will lose his job if the public is not satisfied. Also, the governor's office is not directly involved in administering the child support enforcement program. Consequently, it is more impartial than the child support enforcement agency.

It can also be beneficial to complain to legislators, members of Congress, and even the president. This must be in addition to the appropriate state officials. These officials are not in the chain of command and do not have the power to overturn a decision. They can, however, inquire into the facts of the situation and put a great deal of pressure on the enforcement agency.

One technique that can be very effective is called "shotgunning." This involves making a complaint to several government officials at the same time. For example, a complaint letter can be written to the director of the child support enforcement program, and copies sent to several legislators. Shotgunning can put more pressure on the child support enforcement agency, and it also creates more work. The employee who took the action must draft responses to each of the complaints.

When several complaints are made, they will filter down to the child support enforcement agency at different times. For shotgunning to be most effective, the enforcement agency must know that the father has made several complaints before it responds to the first letter received. This is accomplished by listing all of officials to whom the complaint is being sent on the bottom of each letter. The enforcement agency thus knows that multiple complaints have been made no matter which letter is received first.

The address and telephone number for the child support enforcement program director of each state is included in Appendix A. A state's governor's office can be contacted by writing directly to the state capital.

———●———

Using the Media

The complaint process does not stop with government officials. The media can also be used effectively to halt abuse.

Most local newspapers have "action" or "troubleshooter" columns. Additionally, many local television and radio news stations have segments that are devoted to resolving citizen complaints.

The media process is exactly the same as that for the government. The only difference is the address to which the complaint is sent. The form and content of the complaint should be exactly the same as if it were being sent to a government official.

When a newspaper or television or radio station receives the complaint letter, it is forwarded to the child support enforcement agency for response. The employee who took the action prepares the response, just like any other complaint. The response is then reviewed by superiors and sent back to the newspaper or television station.

This is where the similarity between the government complaint process and the media ends. The purpose of media services is to help find news stories. Both the complaint and the response to the complaint may be printed in the newspaper or discussed on the air. A complaint may even lead to a series of newspaper articles or news segments about the child support enforcement agency. Not only are citizen complaints resolved, many laws and regulations have even been changed as a result of bad press.

Government cannot stand bad press. Most government agencies have public relations staff whose full-time job is to deal with the media. When a complaint is received from a newspaper or television station, extra effort is usually made to resolve the issue.

CHAPTER 12

———●———

A Plan for
the Future

This book provides the knowledge necessary for a father to deal with the child support enforcement system. Knowledge alone, however, is not enough. To be successful, a father must deal with the system. This requires planning now, not tomorrow or the next day.

———●———

Plan for Divorce

Once the decision has been made, planning for divorce should begin as early as possible. Too often, considerations regarding divorce are based upon emotion with little thought toward the future. Parents feel that they "will get along somehow."

The fact of the matter is that most people who get a

divorce cannot afford to do so, which is the real cause of most of their problems afterward. This is why so many women are on welfare; there simply is not enough money to go around after the divorce. Two people cannot live as cheaply as one, but they can live together much more cheaply than living apart and maintaining two separate households.

Parents considering divorce must be aware that they should not do something they can not afford to do. If divorce is not affordable they should wait until they can meet its expense. If they go ahead and do it anyway, there will be problems later. And in our society, the father is often the one who ends up with the problems.

From a financial standpoint, there are three essential steps that must be taken. The first is to pay off the bills. The parents will then be in a much better financial position to afford a divorce. Also, conflict over the terms of the divorce settlement will be reduced. There will be fewer arguments over which parent will be responsible for the debts incurred during the marriage.

Paying off the bills will also reduce a potential liability. While a judge may order one parent to pay the bills it does not mean that the other parent is free of all responsibility. If the parent ordered to pay the bills does not do so, creditors can often collect from the other parent.

The second step is for both parents to become gainfully employed. After the divorce, both parents must work or go on welfare. If the mother is not working, she must get a job before separation occurs. If she has no job skills, she must get the necessary training. It is much less expensive to do so before the divorce.

The third step is to determine what is going to happen to the assets of the marriage. Those assets that are to be sold must be disposed of in an orderly manner in order to get the most money possible. Arrangements must be made to make payments on those assets that are not to be sold. Remember:

divorce is the dissolution of a business partnership. It must be disbanded in such a way as to preserve the value of the business partnership to the greatest possible extent.

Too often, parents end up throwing away the assets that they have worked so many years to accumulate. After the separation, many parents stop making payments on the house and the car. The result is repossession. By the time the divorce is final, there are no assets left to distribute. Both parents lose.

There is always time to plan for divorce. The decision to separate does not happen overnight. It is a result of a series of events that occur over a period of time. Both parents usually know that it is coming, and they should plan for it together, if at all possible.

After the decision to separate has been made, it is still not too late to get the finances in order. Parents think they can no longer live together once they have decided to split up, but in truth in many cases living together for a few more months will not hurt either of them, except in cases of physical abuse. These few months, however, can be critical to the parents' and the children's future.

Once the finances are in order, a magical thing might just happen. The parents may decide that they should not get a divorce after all. A large percentage of marriage break-ups are caused by money problems. The marital difficulties may disappear once the parents get their finances in order.

If the parents are still going to divorce, they must begin developing the terms and conditions to be contained in the decree, which dissolve the business of marriage and distributes the assets and liabilities of the partnership. It also specifies the relationship of the father, mother, and children after the divorce. It is important, therefore, that a great deal of thought be put into the development of the terms and conditions of the divorce decree.

For a father, the terms and conditions relating to the

child support obligation are the most important. If a father obtains a child support obligation that he can live with, and one which clearly specifies what is intended, he may never have any problems.

———●———

Pay Attention

Things do not always turn out as a father would wish. Circumstances can change very unexpectedly, and he can become involved with the child support enforcement agency. Again, planning is the key. A father can determine what the agency can do to him, if he takes the time to examine his own circumstances. He can then take action to prevent disaster from occurring.

Two things work against fathers: poor planning and lack of attention. And two of the most common mistakes are ignoring notices from the child support enforcement agency and inadequate record keeping.

There are many different actions that the child support agency can take against a father. The process by which most of these actions are taken is very much the same. Advance notice is given to the father. If he does not respond to the notice, action is then taken.

Anytime *anything* is received from the child support enforcement agency, the father must take note. When a father receives a notice, he must assume that the action will be taken, and immediately take steps to have the situation resolved. It does not matter whether or not the father is even the right person.

Record keeping is also essential. Fathers should maintain copies of all records pertaining to the divorce, and all documents received from the child support enforcement agency. No one is going to take a father's word. He must be able to prove everything.

As noted previously, the most important records are those that prove a father made his child support payments. These records must be kept for many years. If a father cannot prove he made his child support payments, he may have to pay them over again.

As stated several times throughout this book, fathers should try to put the burden of record keeping for child support payments on someone else, either the clerk of the court or the child support enforcement agency.

---●---

The Role of
the Attorney

There is nothing to prohibit a father from representing himself in any action, including a divorce. It is advisable, though, to retain the services of an attorney if an action involves going to court. However, most fathers are capable of handling other actions, such as responding to notices, negotiating with the child support enforcement agency, and attending informal hearings to determine their child support debt.

An attorney is no substitute for planning on the part of the father. Many people think, when they retain the services of an attorney, that the lawyer will handle it all. An attorney may be of benefit, but he is not going to plan his client's future for him. That a father must do himself.

Additionally, lawyers do make mistakes. Many of the poorly worded divorce decrees are written by them. A father must carefully check everything that his attorney does. If a mistake is made the father is the one who will pay.

The Future

Today, a father can deal with the child support enforcement system, on an individual level, and win. Fathers as a group, however, are losing. Society continues to view the father as the bad guy. He is the cause of poverty of our nation's youth. He has no role in the parent/child relationship after the divorce other than to provide money. The system must be changed.

CHILD SUPPORT OBLIGATIONS

Each year, new child support enforcement laws are being enacted to make more fathers pay. Each year, higher child support schedules are being developed to make those fathers who do pay, pay more. This is happening, in part, because the government is trying to solve the problem of poverty in female-headed households by making more fathers pay extra child support.

More fathers than ever before are now paying child support. The cycle of poverty however, is not being solved. The number of women on welfare is not being reduced. It is a natural reaction on the part of government, therefore, to take even harsher actions against the father to try to solve the problem. It becomes a vicious circle, and treating the symptom does not solve the problem.

Government must be made to recognize that child support is only a symptom of a large, pervasive problem. Fathers should pay child support, but they cannot maintain two households. If the problem is ever to be solved, government must develop programs to enable mothers to become gainfully employed, and require them to work. Welfare reform must become a reality.

CUSTODY AND VISITATION

There must be major changes in the laws and attitudes of judges regarding custody and visitation. They are based upon an outdated concept that the mother is the primary caregiver. She is the one that stays home and provides for the needs of the children. Therefore, she is the one best suited to care for the children after the divorce.

This concept is no longer true. Today, both parents are breadwinners. More than half of all married women with children work, and the percentage is increasing all the time. All single parents must work, or go on welfare. Much of the responsibility of caring for the children is being shifted to day-care centers, which are becoming primary caregivers.

Custody should be awarded to the parent best able to provide for the children. This includes financial support. It should not be awarded to the mother just because she is the mother. In many instances the mother is not in any better position to care for the children than the father. She must work and be away from the children for the same number of hours per day as the father, or go on welfare. Staying home with the children is a luxury that few mothers today can afford.

In cases where the mother is given custody, the father's role in the parent/child relationship must be expanded. He must be given more decision-making authority in shaping his children's future. He must interact more with the children. The role of the father must be more than just brief periods of visitation.

MODIFICATION OF THE DIVORCE DECREE

The laws relating to the modification process must be changed. It is not responsive to the needs of either parent. Fathers so often become victims of the system because they cannot inexpensively modify their child support order on a timely basis. Fathers become so deep in debt that they quit paying altogether, and everyone, especially the children, lose out.

Today, there must be a substantial change in a father's circumstances for him to even qualify for a modification of his obligation. If a father is unemployed for two or three months he may not be able to get the order modified at all. A few months of unemployment may be just enough for financial disaster. The trend is to enact laws that further restrict fathers' rights to modification, rather than trying to help solve the problem.

Even if there is a substantial change in circumstances, it can take several months for a child support order to be modified. In the meantime, a father must pay according to the terms of the original order. This situation is further complicated by the fact that child support orders cannot be modified retroactively. The longer it takes for a child support order to be modified, the worse the father's financial circumstances become. Additionally, he must usually acquire the services of an attorney to have his child support order modified, which is expensive.

A much more responsive mechanism must be developed through which a father can have his child support obligation modified quickly and inexpensively when his financial circumstances change. The best solution would be a system whereby child support obligations are based upon a percentage of income. There would then be no need to modify orders; the child support obligation would change instantaneously when a father's income changed. If it increased, his children would participate. Likewise, a father's child support obligation would decrease when his income decreased.

As discussed in chapter five, it is possible for an individual father to obtain a percentage child support order. This concept would be difficult to sell on a universal basis, however, because percentage orders are hard to enforce. Remember from chapter two that state child support enforcement agencies can be penalized for not efficiently collecting from fathers.

As an alternative, an administrative process could be developed through which fathers could quickly, and inexpensively, have their child support orders modified. The court process is slow and expensive. This is because it is a very general system, and capable of handling anything, from traffic tickets to murder cases. It can handle many different types of cases, but it is not efficient in handling any one of them. Administrative systems (state processes) can be developed for specific purposes and can be very efficient.

A lot of money is spent to collect from fathers. It is time that some money be spent to protect them.

PARENTS' RIGHTS TO MAKE THEIR OWN DECISIONS

Each year, government gains more control over issues relating to separation and divorce. The individual rights of both the mother and the father are being sacrificed for what is seen as the "public good." Rules and regulations are necessary in any society, but the government can go too far. This is what is happening in the child support enforcement program. It must be stopped, or both parents will eventually lose all control over domestic-relations issues after separation occurs.

———————●———————

Changing the System

The system can be changed, but fathers must take the initiative to do it. Changing the system means amending the laws. It also means altering the attitudes of society.

There are just as many fathers as there are mothers. Fathers can put as much pressure on society to change the system as mothers have done. Fathers must do it as a group. There is tremendous power in numbers. Fathers *must* become active members in fathers' rights organizations and they must remain active. Many fathers' rights organizations come and go because fathers lose interest or give up.

Appendix B contains a listing of several state fathers' rights organizations. These organizations often have local chapters. If there is not an organization in the local area, one should be formed. Assistance can be obtained by contacting any established fathers' rights organization.

Once fathers are organized, they must make their cause known. Society must be made aware that a problem exists. The most effective way to accomplish this is through exposure by the media, which is not at all difficult to obtain. Newspapers and television stations are always looking for news stories. The more controversial the issue, the more media attention it gets.

Every opportunity for media exposure must be explored. Reporters should be invited to meetings and rallies, fathers should try to become guests on local talk shows. Press releases should be issued to newspapers. A newsletter should be published and widely distributed.

The objective of the media campaign is to change attitudes. It focuses public attention on the problems that separated and divorced fathers face. It creates a problem that society must solve and an environment in which change can occur.

Changing the system ultimately requires reform of the laws. Fathers, therefore, must become involved in the legislative process. For the most part, this means dealing with the state level. While federal law governs the child support enforcement program, the operational laws regarding divorce, child support, custody, visitation, and so on, are state laws. Most of the laws that must be changed fall under this category.

Fathers' rights organizations must write the necessary legislation and then find legislators to sponsor the laws and get them passed. These groups must also monitor legislation proposed by other organizations, such as the child support enforcement agency.

The key is successful lobbying, which is nothing more than contacting legislators and attempting to convince them to vote a certain way. It is the process through which most legislation passes and fails, and this is where there is real power in numbers. A large organization can put a great deal of pressure on legislators. Imagine legislators getting 10,000 letters from fathers asking them to vote a certain way. Legislators are elected officials, and each letter represents a vote in the next re-election campaign.

Writing letters is only one form of lobbying. Fathers also need direct legislative support for their cause. They must meet with legislators and explain their problems and proposed solutions. They must develop working relationships with legislators and their staffs.

Legislators are accessible. The larger the group or organization, the more accessible they are. Make appointments to talk with them. Invite legislators to speak at meetings. Get them involved. Domestic-relations issues are emotional issues. With a little work, fathers' rights organizations should be able to find many legislators who will become champions of the "father's cause."

Once fathers have a few lawmakers on their side, the legislative staff will assist fathers in preparing the necessary changes in the laws. Additionally, legislators have their own internal system for getting legislation passed. It is called *vote trading*, and it does work.

Lobbying also involves testifying at public hearings. When legislation is proposed, public hearings are held so that interested persons can speak. The testimony given at these hearings influences whether or not the law will be passed. Fathers must attend these hearings and participate.

The system can be changed, but it will not happen overnight. Government moves very slowly. Anyone attempting to make major changes in the law in one swoop is doomed to failure. Success involves making a series of small amendments in the laws over a period of time. The end result is a major change in the system.

All of this sounds like a lot of work, and it is. It also involves becoming involved in an environment that is unfamiliar to most fathers, and somewhat intimidating. It can be done; it has been done.

One of the most successful fathers' rights organizations is the Joint Custody Organization, headquartered in Los Angeles, California. It was founded by James Cook, and has grown into a 2,000-member organization active in forty-three states and fifteen foreign countries.

The Joint Custody Association has been actively involved in addressing most of the issues surrounding separation and divorce, including child support, visitation, custody, and modification. Its primary emphasis, however, has been joint custody, and it has been very effective. Mr. Cook initiated and authored the initial version of California's joint custody statute, and was instrumental in its adoption. Additionally, his organization has facilitated the enactment of joint custody statutes in several other states.

James Cook's organization is not unique; there are many other success stories but there is also a long way to go. Fathers *must* become involved, and stay involved. Nothing worthwhile is ever easy. Nothing is more worthwhile.

APPENDIX A:

Listing of State Child Support Enforcement Agencies

ALABAMA

Director
Bureau of Child Support
Alabama Department of Pensions and Security
64 North Street
Montgomery, Alabama 36130
(205) 261-2872

ALASKA

Director
Child Support Enforcement Division
Department of Revenue
4th Floor
550 West 7th Avenue
Anchorage, Alaska 99501
(907) 276-3441

ARIZONA

Administrator
Child Support Enforcement Administration
Department of Economic Security
P.O. Box 6123—Site Code 776A
Phoenix, Arizona 85005
(602) 255-3465

ARKANSAS

Administrator
Division of Child Support Enforcement
Arkansas Social Services
P.O. Box 3358
Little Rock, Arkansas 72203
(501) 371-2464

CALIFORNIA

Chief
Child Support Program Management Branch
Department of Social Services
744 P Street Mail Stop 9-011
Sacramento, California 95814
(916) 322-8495

COLORADO

Director
Division of Child Support Enforcement
Department of Social Services
717 17th Street
P.O. Box 181000
Denver, Colorado 80218-0899
(303) 294-5994

CONNECTICUT

Director
Bureau of Child Support Enforcement

Department of Human Resources
1049 Asylum Avenue
Hartford, Connecticut 06105
(203) 566-3053

DELAWARE

Director
Division of Child Support Enforcement
Department of Health and Social Services
P.O. Box 904
New Castle, Delaware 19720
(302) 421-8300

DISTRICT OF COLUMBIA

Chief
Office of Paternity and Child Support Enforcement
Department of Human Services
3rd Floor—Suite 3013
425 I Street, N.W.
Washington, D.C. 20009
(202) 724-5610

FLORIDA

Director
Office of Child Support Enforcement
Department of Health and Rehabilitative Services
1317 Winewood Boulevard—Bldg 3
Tallahassee, Florida 32399-0700
(904) 488-9900

GEORGIA

Director
Office of Child Support Recovery

State Department of Human Resources
P.O. Box 80000
Atlanta, Georgia 30357
(404) 894-4119

GUAM

Supervisor
Child Support Enforcement Office
Department of Public Health and Social Services
California First Bank Building
194 Hernan Cortez Avenue, 2nd Floor
Agana, Guam 96910
(671) 477-2036

HAWAII

Director
Child Support Enforcement Agency
Department of Attorney General
770 Kapiolani Boulevard—Suite 703
Honolulu, Hawaii 96813
(808) 548-5779

IDAHO

Chief
Bureau of Child Support Enforcement
Department of Health and Welfare
Statehouse Mail
Boise, Idaho 83720
(208) 334-5710

ILLINOIS

Chief
Bureau of Child Support Enforcement

Illinois Department of Public Aid
Jesse B. Harris Building
P.O. Box 2127
100 South Grand Avenue East
Springfield, Illinois 62705
(217) 782-1366

INDIANA

Director
Child Support Enforcement Division
Department of Public Welfare
4th Floor
141 South Merridian Street
Indianapolis, Indiana 46225
(317) 232-4885

IOWA

Chief
Bureau of Collections
Iowa Department of Human Services
Hoover Building—5th Floor
Des Moines, Iowa 50319
(515) 281-5580

KANSAS

Director
Child Support Enforcement Program
Department of Social and Rehabilitation Services
2700 West Sixth
1st Floor, Perry Building
Topeka, Kansas 66606
(913) 296-3237

KENTUCKY

Director
Division of Child Support Enforcement

Department of Social Insurance
Cabinet for Human Resources
6th Floor East
275 East Main Street
Frankfort, Kentucky 40621
(502) 564-2285

LOUISIANA

Director
Support Enforcement Services Program
Office of Family Security
Department of Health and Human Resources
P.O. Box 94065
Baton Rouge, Louisiana 70804
(504) 342-4780

MAINE

Director
Support Enforcement and Location Unit
Bureau of Social Welfare
Department of Human Services
State House, Station 11
Augusta, Maine 04333
(207) 289-2886

MARYLAND

Executive Director
Child Support Enforcement Administration
Department of Human Resources
11 East Mount Royal Avenue
Baltimore, Maryland 21201
(301) 333-3978

MASSACHUSETTS

Deputy Commissioner
Department of Revenue

Child Support Enforcement Division
215 First Street
Cambridge, Massachusetts 02142
(617) 621-4200

MICHIGAN

Director
Office of Child Support
Department of Social Services
Suite 621
300 South Capital Avenue
Lansing, Michigan 48909
(517) 373-7570

MINNESOTA

Director
Office of Child Support
Department of Human Services
Suite 403
Metro Square Building
St. Paul, Minnesota 55101
(612) 296-2499

MISSISSIPPI

Director
Child Support Division
State Department of Public Welfare
P.O. Box 352
515 East Amite Street
Jackson, Mississippi 39205
(601) 354-0341, ext. 503

MISSOURI

Administrator
Division of Child Support Enforcement

Department of Social Services
P.O. Box 1527
Jefferson City, Missouri 65102-1527
(314) 751-4301

MONTANA

Director
Child Support Enforcement Program
Department of Revenue
Investigation and Enforcement Division
Helena, Montana 59604
(406) 444-4614

NEBRASKA

Administrator
Child Support Enforcement Office
Department of Social Services
P.O. Box 95026
Lincoln, Nebraska 68509
(402) 471-9125

NEVADA

Chief
Child Support Enforcement Program
Department of Human Resources
2527 North Carson Street, Capital Complex
Carson City, Nevada 89710
(702) 885-4744

NEW HAMPSHIRE

Administrator
Office of Child Support Enforcement Services
Division of Welfare

Health and Welfare Building
Hazen Drive
Concord, New Hampshire 03301
(603) 271-4426

NEW JERSEY

Director
Child Support and Paternity Unit
Department of Human Services
CN 716
Trenton, New Jersey 08625
(609) 538-2401

NEW MEXICO

Chief
Child Support Enforcement Bureau
Department of Human Services
P.O. Box 2348—PERA Building
Sante Fe, New Mexico 87503
(505) 827-4230

NEW YORK

Director
Office of Child Support Enforcement
New York State Department of Social Services
P.O. Box 14
1 Commerce Plaza
Albany, New York 12260
(518) 474-9081

NORTH CAROLINA

Chief
Child Support Enforcement Section

Division of Social Services
Department of Human Resources
433 North Harrington Street
Raleigh, North Carolina 27603-1393
(919) 733-4120

NORTH DAKOTA

Administrator
Child Support Enforcement Agency
North Dakota Department of Human Services
State Capital
Bismark, North Dakota 58505
(701) 224-3582

OHIO

Chief
Bureau of Child Support
Ohio Department of Human Services
State Office Tower—27th Floor
30 East Broad Street
Columbus, Ohio 43266-0423
(614) 466-3233

OKLAHOMA

Administrator
Child Support Enforcement Unit
Department of Human Services
P.O. Box 25352
Oklahoma City, Oklahoma 73125
(405) 424-5871

OREGON

Director
Recovery Services Section

Adult and Family Services Division
Department of Human Resources
P.O. Box 14506
Salem, Oregon 97309
(503) 378-5439

PENNSYLVANIA

Director
Bureau of Child Support Enforcement
Department of Public Welfare
P.O. Box 8018
Harrisburg, Pennsylvania 17105
(717) 787-3672

PUERTO RICO

Director
Child Support Enforcement Program
Department of Social Services
Call Box 3349
San Juan, Puerto Rico 00904
(809) 722-4731

RHODE ISLAND

Chief Supervisor
Bureau of Family Support
Department of Human Services
77 Dorrance Street
Providence, Rhode Island 02903
(401) 277-2409

SOUTH CAROLINA

Executive Assistant
Child Support Enforcement Division

Department of Social Services
P.O. Box 1520
Columbia, South Carolina 29202-9988
(803) 737-9938

SOUTH DAKOTA

Program Administrator
Office of Child Support Enforcement
Department of Social Services
700 Governors Drive
Pierre, South Dakota 57501-2291
(605) 773-3641

TENNESSEE

Director
Child Support Services
Department of Human Services
Citizens Plaza Building—12th Floor
400 Deadrick Street
Nashville, Tennessee 37219
(615) 741-1820

TEXAS

Special Assistant Attorney General
Child Support Enforcement Division
Office of Attorney General
P.O. Box 12548
Austin, Texas 78711-2548
(512) 463-2181

UTAH

Director
Office of Recovery Services

Department of Social Services
120 North 200 West
P.O. Box 45011
Salt Lake City, Utah 84145-0011
(801) 538-4402

VERMONT

Director
Child Support Division
Department of Social Welfare
103 South Main Street
Waterbury, Vermont 05676
(802) 241-2868

VIRGIN ISLANDS

Chief
Support and Paternity Division
Department of Law
46 Norre Gade
St. Thomas, Virgin Islands 00801
(809) 776-0372

VIRGINIA

Director
Division of Support Enforcement
Department of Social Services
8004 Franklin Farms Drive
Richmond, Virginia 23288
(804) 662-9297

WASHINGTON

Director
Revenue Division

Department of Social and Health Services
P.O. Box 9162 Mail Stop PI-11
Olympia, Washington 98504
(206) 459-6488

WEST VIRGINIA

Assistant Commissioner
Office of Child Support Enforcement
Department of Human Services
1900 Washington Street, East
Charleston, West Virginia 25305
(304) 348-3780

WISCONSIN

Director
Division of Community Services
Office of Child Support
1 West Wilson St., Room 385
P.O. Box 7851
Madison, Wisconsin 53707-7851
(608) 266-1175

WYOMING

Program Manager
Child Support Enforcement Section
Division of Public Assistance and Social Services
State Department of Health and Social Services
Hathaway Building
Cheyenne, Wyoming 82002
(307) 777-7892

APPENDIX B:

Listing of Fathers' Rights Organizations

Arizona

Arizona Fathers Demanding Equal Justice
1544 East Jarvis
Mesa, Arizona 85204
(602) 835-7906

California

POPCO
6039 Rancho Mission Road
Building 5, No. 103
San Diego, California 92108
(619) 283-2512

Fathers of America
P.O. Box 3075
Santa Monica, California 90403
(213) 822-3517

Joint Custody Association
10606 Wilkins Avenue
Los Angeles, California 90024
(213) 475-5352

United Fathers of America
415 North Sycamore Street
Suite 207
Santa Ana, California 92701
(714) 542-5624

Connecticut

Divorced Men's Association of Connecticut
31 Daniel Street
East Hartford, Connecticut 06118
(203) 528-0526

Delaware

Male Parents for Equal Rights
10 Downing Street
New Castle, Delaware 19720
(302) 571-8383

District of Columbia

National Congress of Men
2020 Pennsylvania Avenue, NW
Suite 277
Washington, D.C. 20006
(202) FATHERS

Florida

United Fathers, Inc.
5557 NW
194 Lane
Miami, Florida 33055
(305) 265-0599

Illinois

The Parental Rights Organization
3500 West Church Street, Suite 108
Evanston, Illinois 60203-1637

American Society of Separated and Divorced Men
575 Keep Street
Elgin, Illinois 60120
(312) 695-2200

Iowa

Fathers for Equal Rights
3623 Douglas
Des Moines, Iowa 50310
(515) 277-8789 and (515) 233-1077

Kansas

Fathers Demanding Equal Justice
689 South Mission Road
Wichita, Kansas 67207
(316) 686-5871

Louisiana

Concerned Parents for Children's Rights
313 Almo Street
Lake Charles, Louisiana 70601
(318) 433-0504

Massachusetts

Concerned Fathers
P.O. Box 2768
Springfield, Massachusetts 01101
(413) 736-7432

Michigan

Fathers for Equal Rights
25339 Lois Lane Drive
Southfield, Michigan 48075
(313) 354-3080

Minnesota

Men's Rights Association
Route 6
Forest Lake, Minnesota 55025

R-Kids
P.O. Box 9816
North St. Paul, Minnesota 55109
(612) 770-6164

Missouri

Fathers Demanding Equal Justice for Children
P.O. Box 398
Columbia, Missouri 65205

New Hampshire

Fathers United for Equal Justice
Box 45
78 Portsmouth Avenue
New Castle, New Hampshire 03854
(603) 436-8810

New Jersey

Fathers United for Equal Rights
P.O. Box 2340
Elizabeth, New Jersey 07207
(201) 969-3741

New Mexico

Dads Against Discrimination
P.O. Box 1273
Albuquerque, New Mexico 87103
(505) 299-COPE and (505) 299-2673

New York

Coalition of Free Men
P.O. Box 129
Manhasset, New York 11030
(516) 482-6378

Fathers' Rights Association of New York
3715 Brewerton Road
North Syracuse, New York 13212
(315) 455-7043

North Carolina

Fathers United for Equal Rights
P.O. Box 51405
Raleigh, North Carolina 27609
(919) 846-1380

Ohio

Fathers and Children for Equity (FACES)
P.O. Box 766
Worthington, Ohio 43085
(614) 275-6767

Ohio Fathers' Family Rights Association
P.O. Box 565, Forest Park Branch
Dayton, Ohio 45405
(513) 277-5151

Pennsylvania

Father's and Children's Equality
P.O. Box 117
Drexel Hill, Pennsylvania 19026

Texas

Texas Fathers for Equal Rights
P.O. Box 50052
One Main Place Station
Dallas, Texas 75250
(214) 934-3885

Texas Fathers for Equal Rights
P.O. Box 61249
Houston, Texas 77208
(703) 960-0407

Utah

Utah Parents for Children's Rights
6260 West Lilac Drive
West Jorden, Utah 84984

Virginia

Fathers United for Equal Rights
7710 Jansen Drive
Springfield, Virginia 22152
(703) 451-9321

Washington

United Fathers of America
Suite 1523 Smith Tower
Seattle, Washington 98104
(206) 623-5050

West Virginia

West Virginia Fathers for Equal Rights
12 Woodland Drive
Beverly, West Virginia 26253
(304) 636-6261

Index